ART & EGO

Edward Rozzo is a photographer and teacher. His professional photography for major multi-national industries has taken him throughout Europe. He has taught in Italy, Switzerland, and Belgium and is now professor of Visual Culture Studies at the Bocconi University in Milan, Italy. He also teaches Retail Semiotics at the Ecole Superieure d'Arts Appliqués in Vevey, Switzerland.

Marcus Reichert is a painter and a poet who has also worked in film. His filmworks are held in the Archive of the Museum of Modern Art, New York. *Reichert: The Human Edifice* by Mel Gooding, with 100 photographs by the artist in colour, is published by Artmedia Press, London and *Displaced Person: Poetry, Pornography & Politics* (Selected Writings 1970-2005) is published by Ziggurat Books, London.

Simon Lane is the author of four novels, *Le Veilleur*, *Still-life With Books*, *Fear*, and *Word of Mouth*. He has written for a wide variety of publications in Europe and the United States, and has worked in film, radio, and television both as a writer and an actor. Born in England, he has lived in London, Berlin, Milan, New York, and Paris. He now lives and works in Rio de Janeiro.

ART & EGO

Marcus Reichert
in conversation with
Edward Rozzo

ZIGGURAT BOOKS
PSI Publishing, St. Quentin House, Fitzhugh Grove,
London SW18 3SE

Enquiries: zigguratedditions@orange.fr (Ziggurat Books)

Front cover photo: Marcus Reichert by Edward Rozzo
Back cover photo: Self-Portrait by Edward Rozzo

Printed by Biddles Ltd., King's Lynn, Norfolk

Distributed by Art Books International
15 Windmill Grove
Portchester
Hampshire PO16 9HT
England

T: +44 (0)2392 200 080
F: +44 (0)2392 200 090
email: sales@art-bks.com

First Edition

ISBN 978-0-9546656-5-4

ACKNOWLEDGMENTS

We would like to thank the following for their very kind support and guidance: R & R Publications, Stephen Barber, Alexandra Batsford, Katrina del Mar, Philip-Lorca diCorcia, David Douglas Duncan, Winston Eggleston, Piers Faccini, Michelle Franco, Nan Goldin, Laura Hajar, Michael Hoppen, Simon Lane, Mark Luscombe-Whyte, Bryony McLennan, Samer Mohdad, Roy Oxlade, Lauren Panzo, Martin Parr, Laura Pollini, Anna Pryer, Leslie Simitich, Oliviero Toscani, Christina Turley, Mike von Joel, Kristin Ware, Ron Warren, Cara Weston, Mme Gilberte Brassaï, who died in 2005, and especially our editor, Sally MacLeod.

MR & ER

CONTENTS

THE DIALOGUE
Foreward by Simon Lane

"Fear you not my part of the dialogue."
Much Ado About Nothing
William Shakespeare

Some people talk a lot, some talk less. Some hum, some sing. Some might whistle, like birds or busy joiners. We don't know what we sound like and, when we hear our voices from a recording, we start at the words of a stranger. This discrepancy, between perception and reality, is part of us, symbolized by the erroneous image we carry of ourselves in perpetuity: the asymmetrical face that greets us within the square, the circle, of the looking glass, as we arise from the disquiet or wistful pleasure of our dreams. Happy aliens, we fly through the business of life inured to our own, fictional nature. The only truth we have at our disposal is hidden within us; unless, of course, we elect to share it with others. An identical twin would at least have a reasonable likeness available to him, if his other half were to hand; if not, just like the singular version of the genus, he would simply rely on what is known in Francophonia as La toile d'araignee du monde. So, here it is, a modest thread of communication about to be swished up the Atlantic to my trusty correspondent, the polymath, Marcus Reichert, at work no doubt, or at rest, in his home in the Cévennes. Yes, "the web of the spider of the world," clumsy enough inversion for opposing hemispheres as I tap my way to print 23 degrees south in Rio de Janeiro, a window rattling in a storm.

Conversation is dialogue without which we would be even lonelier than we think. Men are islands, archipelagos, chartable if not always charitable. For the most part, our lives consist of an inaudible dialogue held between the self and its partner, call the latter a conscience, perhaps the devil's advocate, in order to make the former more rounded, more sensible; unless of course we enter into dialogue with others, in which case a certain harmony, not to say order, is engendered. Even then, the inner voice persists, checking, unchecking, what we have said, what we will say, regretting a slip of the tongue, relishing a turn of phrase if we are fortunate to discover one within the circuitous metaphor of discourse.

All artists talk to themselves. It is a given. And their art is the consequence of this peculiar dialogue. Art in all its forms is the suspect translation of thought into action, a daunting enough task in the best of circumstances, what my friend, the painter, Brett Whiteley, called "difficult pleasure." The truth may well exist yet everything is consigned to an uneasy approximation in which, given the right touch, mystery might hold sway. No harm in striving for lucidity, however, as the processes of conception and execution are but part of dialogue's equation. After all, there is the reader, the viewer, to consider as well, and that person will also be obliged to create a dialogue in order to make sense of the work, the picture, the painting, in question. No, it is not just the artists who are mad enough to talk to themselves; the whole wide world is at it!

Marcus Reichert and Edward Rozzo have instigated a dialogue which includes the exploration of specific themes, while the images chosen by each are starting points rather than illustrations, intensely personal selections which travel from the fierce, uncompromising realism of mortality and war to the simple charms offered within this, our mortal coil. They introduce themselves as exiles, explaining their American roots in life and art, revealing both intimacy and objectivity, before going on to exchange ideas on many other subjects: dislocation in general; tantalization; the ignoble descent of art to fashion; the power, or impotency, of art to shock the viewer, either through immediate, natural reality or distant violence; technical and emotional concerns with regard to film and photography, such as the evocative, nostalgic power of monochrome;

cultural anarchy in which it is suggested that consumerism has effectively consumed us all; and man's apparent addiction to the arachnid's sticky labour. If art is a game, the images, meanwhile, happily break the rules for the reader, teasing emotion from a wildly ranging aesthetic. Who can argue with a corpse on a battlefield? And who could forego a smile at the diminutive Spaniard in those magnificent Y-fronts? From the anonymity of extinction to the celebration of life itself, the image, to twist the metaphor and break another rule, has the last word, while the ongoing, rapid interview sustains the barrage of the senses, the mind.

The subject of ego, of course, is intrinsic to the dialogue. As Reichert says, "I paint to demonstrate to myself that I am actually alive," a serious enough admission. Pingo ergo sum! The nature of the artist is thus equated with the nature of the art, the ego of those who dare to talk aloud as compared to the product of their musings. But the observer must never be ignored, even if most artists and writers go about their work for their own salvation, personal, material. After all, paintings, photographs, pictures in general, invite a dialogue of their own in which the object and the viewer may pleasantly agree or disagree yet, like music, may not actually exist behind closed doors. Consent is always the proof of good art, lending a moment of silence to the proceedings. Thankfully, "dialogue" is not something limited, as many would have it, to two people. On the contrary. According to the dictionary, it may consist of "a conversation between two or more persons," even "a person and something else," the "di" not "two" in this instance but simply the first syllable of the Greek word "dialogesthai," meaning "to speak across" or "converse," something for which we should all be extremely grateful.

Rio de Janeiro
27th September 2007

1.

MR: Both you and I were born and raised in the United States. My impression is that culturally your family was predominately Italian in character. My grandfather spoke German (and English) and when I was little my mother had the help of a Mennonite woman who also spoke German. My mother often referred to her French Catholic background, she also referred to her father's Englishness. I never knew her parents. You left for Italy long before I settled in England. This seemed your determination soon after you and I met at the age of 18. You may recall that when we met, I'd already spent time in Paris and painted more like a European than an American. Your photographs of those years often made me long for the intimacy I'd found in France. I recall you being particularly fond of the work of Josef Koudelka. We've spent most of our lives in Europe and certainly this has greatly influenced the way we think and work.

ER: You and I have had the privilege of understanding more than one culture and that puts us in a position to understand a few more things than some who have never lived abroad. I can only say, though, that it's a bit frightening when you see how difficult cross-cultural communication really is. As to Josef Koudelka, I was attracted by his gypsy work because I found it so humane, so open to a way of life which seemed so far away from my own. I wanted to save the world too, with my photography I wanted to be part of showing the Family of Man to the rest of the world. Very romantic, very '68 or very post-war, if you will. Fortunately, I haven't become a cynic which is the usual reaction to being romantic in your youth. You eventually see the world as it is and you just give up, condemning right and left. I've become more tolerant and I'm still a bit romantic. I even have high hopes for America.

Just to get the record straight, I was brought up in and around New York City. My father was the son of Italian immigrants, my mother the daughter of a horse-raising family from Quebec. I've lived in Italy since the early '70s and my wife is French. My children were both born in Italy, so I can say that we are pretty well cross-cultured. But then again, everything is of European origin which makes us, from a certain point of view, very provincial!

MR: But how do you think being a European—one who has been transplanted from America—has affected the way you see as a photographer, as an artist? Do you believe you see differently now (after all these years), do you believe you see differently than you would had you remained in America?

ER: It's a funny thing, but I think I see more as an American than as a European despite the fact that I've spent my whole adult life living and working in Europe. I think my *thinking* has changed quite a bit, but my imagery, my photography, the way I go about thinking about art, that all, I believe, is very American. Place, in this sense, is injected into your mental habits. I could never say what I would have done if I had stayed in the United States, but I can surely say that I feel my mental structure is quite American. I've assimilated an enormous amount of things from living in Europe, but the framework in which you learn what the world is about stays with you for your life. I personally think that your work is very American, do you?

MR: First, I have to ask how you think an American sees, as opposed, let's say, to an Italian, or any other European for that matter?

ER: Well, that's a very good question. I can only throw my accumulated feelings and intuitions at you. I think Europeans choose subject matter which is usually more tied up with history, politics, and literal thinking. I think Europeans for the most part are very literal, they thrive on the spoken word, and most of the time their visual work reflects that. I think Americans, on the other hand, are more *naïf.* I think they play with colours much more than Europeans, I think they play in general much more than Europeans. There's more joking, juxtapositioning, casualness. Europeans are generally more serious in their attitude, they take themselves more seriously. I find Americans are less ideological, less political, more prone to follow an instinct, fool around with an idiom. Of course, there are millions of exceptions, but these are the characteristics that usually emerge, therefore the American vision appeals more to a global audience.

MR: I doubt the global relevance of much of what is created visually in America. I would never deny its power, especially not its power to transform the aesthetics of other cultures, but I'm not at all certain that *the big concept* is anything but that. It may sound elitist, but my craving has always been for greater sophistication in what I am obliged to appreciate visually. Pastiche seems to suffice in American visual culture, whereas it hardly exists in Europe. As long as something looks like something that has already succeeded, it can pass for some sort of equivalent. I find this extremely irritating. I wonder if Martin Scorsese's sense of style would be quite so operatic if he hadn't grown up in Little Italy. His shifts from scene to scene are poetical, as his images accumulate meaning, and conversely eradicate or, even more astoundingly, reverse it. This comes, I think, from observing a particular kind of behaviour at close hand, and that can only occur in an environment where language and gesture articulate thought. America is a faddish culture, it inadvertently obliterates originality. So, it takes a huge effort to get anyone's attention, ask Julian Schnabel.

ER: What has been so enriching about living in Italy for almost 40 years is the intellectual stimulation, the profound richness of Western culture, philosophy, and history that permeates almost any conversation you have (except those concerning soccer). I feel immensely privileged to have been exposed to this kind of intellectual culture. Growing up in New York City meant being street smart, watching out where you were going and who was around you so as to avoid danger. You had to be cool and stay on top of what was happening. It took me quite a few years to start thinking more and reacting less.

MR: When you ask if I think my work is American in character, I have to say emphatically *no*. But, in many ways, that's a foolish thing to say, because when it came to making serious paintings I can't deny that I was influenced by the Abstract Expressionists, like Arshile Gorky and Willem deKooning. However, their work derived from European modernity, especially Picasso. The most interesting painters of my generation, I feel, are immersed in reckoning with the weight of European sensibility that formed them, people like George Condo, Sandro Chia, Marlene Dumas, Peter Doig, Julian Schnabel, etc. Even David Salle's work appears to me to be filtered through a sticky veil of European sophistication. To put it as bluntly as I can, there wouldn't have been an Andy Warhol without there first having been an Henri Matisse. Perhaps all of this is thuddingly obvious to most people who really look at painting. When it comes to the photographs I take, they were taken all over the Western world, so they're not about any one society or culture, and they were never intended for anyone to see anyway. My photographs now being seen by the public is just plain freakish, but I can't say I didn't encourage that possibility.

I would like to go back to sense of place as it pertains to our visual relationship with our immediate environment, both past and present. In Mauro Fiorese's 2005 interview, you say:

"For years I've been slowly working on understanding my relationship with society, which has brought me to continually photograph things which I feel reveal some of the feelings within this relationship. This void found within the present is just one of the possibilities of reading the complexity of contemporary society. I don't intend it to be the only interpretation, nor necessarily a privileged one, but you've got to start somewhere and this phrase, *la lacuna del presente*, struck me.

It's a phrase spoken by Remo Bodei[1] in an interview with Gianni Vattimo which refers to the overwhelming possibilities given to us by industrial society, through the media, through images and words, to be simultaneously in touch with more and more global events. But instead of widening our experience, ironically, more often than not, these expanding possibilities lead to a kind of deadening of our senses through overstimulation. That's a very interesting part of the contemporary experience. I find it ever so present in those moments of introspection when you ask yourself, 'Where am I going? Why?'

Therefore, I could say that many moments of our lives are spent looking backwards towards a reassuring, though subjectively fictitious past or, depending on our weaknesses, looking forward with fragile hope in order to avoid the surge of anxiety which fills the present. Looking for visual expressions which underline some of the void the present retains has therefore become part of my research."

Several things occurred to me as I read this which you may or may not find relevant, mostly because my response to much of what you say hinges on personal experience. My instinct has always been to stand outside society looking in. In this way, I realise an objectivity that enables me to express myself without being terribly concerned about the consequences. Perhaps this could be interpreted as an understandable compulsion on my part, because I was allowed so seldom to express myself in the context of my family. I occupy, if you will, a void which could be your *lacuna del presente*. There are no guidelines within this void, and therefore the images I make often appear, I imagine, to have very little relationship to society.

---

[1] Remo Bodei, Professor of History, Pisa University, Pisa; *Filosofia al Presente*, Gianni Vattimo, Garzanti, 1990 (Conversations with Remo Bodei and others); also *Destini Personali: l'età della colonizzazione delle coscienze*, Remo Bodei, Feltrinelli, 2004

ER: I've read[2] that our relationship with a projected world is the outcome of our relationship to the caretakers in the beginning of our life. That is, the presence or absence of being included emotionally alters your perspective on *where* you are throughout your life. The basic trust you share with your caretakers as an infant (no matter who they may have been) determines your organisation of space and time which invariably is linked with the projection of self. So it's very common for people to feel as if they are in a movie, looking at society but not being a part of it. It's part of a general dissociation which is primarily emotional and then, through projection, a personal reality. In a certain sense, we *all* feel like we're outside society looking in.

MR: The "surge of anxiety which fills the present" is unavoidable, felt publicly and privately, and a direct result of the inevitability of, firstly, death and, secondly, the haphazard destruction meted out by humanity. I find re-negotiating the past nearly impossible, and am now convinced that the *anxious* pleasure people take in the anticipation of violence will continue to infect the future. Although visual expressions of this void would also seem inevitable, your research and exposition of this state strikes me as uncanny, especially when so many artists are striving so mightily to find some palatable universal expression of their existence.

As I have lived in quite a few different societies and tend to regard the human edifice as one disparate conglomeration of people after another, I find it extremely difficult to cling to the aesthetic precepts of any one society—believe me, I know they are there. In fact, upon confronting many manifestations of what any one contemporary society might find acceptably stimulating, I cringe. Undoubtedly, some people cringe when they gaze upon my painting, perhaps less so my photography (for reasons of universality). For me, the overstimulation you

---

[2] *Modernity and Self-identity: Self and Society in the Late Modern Age*, Anthony Giddens, Polity Press, Cambridge, 1991

refer to has most to do with the sheer numbers of people and things in the world and the aggressiveness with which we are asked to recognise them.

ER: We really should analyse what that means. Do you want to get into that or should we get back to the transformation of place?

MR: Right now, I'd rather examine our response to *place* and how that might affect our state of mind as it relates to image-making. Perhaps we could take on the issue of violence as it pertains to image-making and its impact on the viewer in another discussion.

I feel very strongly that there is an almost contradictory aspect of *universality* in the mind of the photographer; that is, the photographer who takes pictures in the real world rather than staging his images. As I enjoy all sorts of indulgences and particularly, in this instance, my voyeuristic tendency, I am excited by alien environments. Bars are especially attractive to me because one is allowed to observe all sorts of human behaviour at close range with impunity. But, getting back to the *contradictory* bit, I am essentially a recluse and seldom go farther afield than another village 30 minutes down the road. I have always chosen to live among people who have no idea where I really came from—there's no way they could know, and what's the point of telling them? So I photograph my immediate environment as if it were a foreign place, at least that's how it strikes me. When I came across a book of William Eggleston's photographs—this would have been in North Carolina in 1993 or 1994—I was fascinated by the sensation of the images being outside the generic consciousness of the place in which they were taken. His photographs had the *otherness* that I find essential to the excitement of taking pictures. I'm curious to know if this is true for you, or if you find the sort of excitement I'm describing only when in an unfamiliar place.

ER: You obviously take a personal pleasure in seeing images of places where the metaphysical seems to prevail over the real. Eggleston's photographs are also about the beauty of detail, or hyper-reality if you wish. They're about colour. His images cover such a range of subject matter, though, that it's not easy to pinpoint his way of seeing. I find his work indicative of the way thousands of photographers from our generation see the world, but I must confess that it doesn't move me much. I must also confess that I haven't looked closely enough at his work and I only know the most published of his images. So, to be fair, I'm in no position to voice my opinion. I know Szarkowski[3] thought the world of him, which says quite a bit about his worth. Anyway, any *new* place is exciting because you see everything. Your vision isn't used to anything there, so everything has the same value, like *gestalt* analysis. I find that exciting, although it's harder and harder to find a place on the earth which seems *unfamiliar*. Globalisation has just about flattened the visual aspect of most industrialised cities and nations. But I crave examining things which *are* local. At least they are unfamiliar!

MR: Yes, a paradox that continues to astound me. It's a cliché, but it's that moment when you are standing in your bathroom, which you've stood in a million times, and for no particular reason the soap resting in its hollow in the sink somehow communicates our mortality and the ever so fragile intimacy of our lives. In this moment, perhaps the *metaphysical*, as you call it, does transform the real. And so, nothing is familiar in that moment, we are suspended in time and place, like tadpoles. For me, the photographs that have the greatest meaning are those that communicate this suspension of time and place. They have about them an eternality that transcends the moment, that perhaps *is* the moment. But these are the very best photographs.

---

[3] John Szarkowski, Director, Department of Photography, Museum of Modern Art, New York (1962-1991); *The Photographer's Eye*, MoMA Publication, New York, 1963

2.

ER: I've always had a very complex relationship with taking photographs of nude women. I found hard pornography exciting as a teenager, but as you grow into different relationships it's always a cheap substitute for the real thing.

MR: I came to realise somewhere along the line that my view of women as sexual creatures had been formed largely by the images that had excited me sexually as a kid. I wasn't hooked on pornography—it really wasn't available at the time—but I was hooked on a kind of inaccessible perfection that dominated this sort of published imagery. It didn't matter to me whether it was lurid or ethereal, just as long as it gave me something to think about. When I finally came to know women sexually, I found the reality of those encounters very disheartening. I'd become an idealist, and that was perverse. It was especially perverse when I realised that I had an enormous amount of affection for someone but wasn't interested in her sexually at all. I was living in a jungle of pornographic images in my mind that I would never realise, unless of course I moved into what I had been conditioned to know as forbidden territory. But I soon realised that some women know what this is all about, and then it all became more interesting.

ER: When I take a photograph of a nude woman, it's always the woman I'm in love with at the moment. It's always my companion, because photographing another woman nude is almost like making love to her, and that's not my way of doing things. When I do take photographs of my companion nude, I want the image to have that raw feeling of natural sex which makes the actual relationship so rewarding. I don't want a perfect body, with predictable curves and taut nipples. I want to feel the flesh, the individuality of the body. I'm interested in the defects that make that woman so particular. I want to smell how *special* she is. Unfortunately, for just these reasons my women companions usually don't want to be photographed by me. The problem is that they are sold on a comic book idea of what they should look like.

MR: I don't like photographs of men making love to women. I don't like another man interfering in my relationship with the woman in the picture. It's impossible for me to pretend I'm the guy in the photograph. Similarly, I don't like a mirror in the bedroom, or whichever room we happen to be in at the time, because seeing myself in the act somehow ruins it for me. I find it distracting in the extreme. It brings an element of mortality into play that has to do with the two of us being objectified by the image in the mirror. We're no longer me and her, we're now *him* and her. Our bodies have become one with the furnishing. Observing a woman looking at herself in a mirror is another matter altogether.

ER: That gets back to John Berger's insight[4] about women being looked at and men *and* women doing the looking. There is a kind of equilibrium between visual excitement and emotion, between what you think is happening and what really is. If this weren't the case, it wouldn't make any difference who you were sleeping with. Late modernity has transformed personal sexual habits into a tribal cult, shoving all of us into various moulds and making it harder and harder to stay emotionally in touch. As with all our technological solutions, every aspect of copulation has been separated, studied, and evaluated. Size, weight, attitude, life-style. You can't be a real person, you have to be fit. Tanned. Muscular. Full in the right places, not in the wrong ones. And the orgasm has been institutionalised: how long, when, where does it originate, did you enjoy it? *Did you enjoy it?* What kind of question is that?

MR: A little too personal for my taste, and I don't care who's asking it. Perhaps if a professional lady were asking it, I'd be

---

[4] *Ways of Seeing*, John Berger, Penguin Books, London, 1990 and *About Looking*, John Berger, Vintage Books, New York, 1992

flattered. You are probably aware that prostitutes refuse to be kissed on the mouth. It's an unwritten law: you do not kiss a prostitute on the mouth. The prostitute's job is to bring the client to orgasm. Evidently, it is meant to be just that simple. I nearly got thrown out of a servicing establishment in New York for talking to the girl I'd chosen rather than getting on with the work at hand. She had a husband and two children, which I found interesting. Her husband had a perfectly good job, nevertheless she was determined to be self-reliant. It was when I asked her what she did with her money that she buzzed for the attendant. I wasn't there to be brought to orgasm, I was there to see if I might find someone to photograph, someone who would submit without inhibition to my camera. Obviously, I failed. I did have better luck however with a girl I met on the subway, but she wanted to be paid and I didn't have any money.

ER: I think Edward Weston's nudes are cold, and yet he was a real womaniser. His vegetables however are very erotic. The famous pepper image was even censored in the 1930's as pornographic. But his photographs of women are prudish. Mapplethorpe's flowers are profoundly homo-erotic. It's hard to find images of women that are profoundly erotic. Most are clichéd and plastic. Lee Friedlander's nudes remind me of mine. They're real—real women, real sex. I love them.

MR: My nudes tend to be enigmatic, perhaps because I find people without their clothes enigmatic. It's most often the place I'm in with someone that inspires me to photograph that person naked, or nearly naked. I find the human body simply naked, without any extenuating circumstances in frame, not very interesting. I'm much more excited by the idea that we're taking pictures in a given place at a given time and this is—intimately—what we're about. But there is a formality to how I take a picture that often freezes the plasticity of the moment. In other words, I defeat the moment by imposing myself upon it. I don't think this is a particularly good thing, and I'm not as tempted as I used to be to invade the privacy of my own life.

You mentioned that a photograph by Oliviero Toscani of a new-born child was banned in England. It was considered by the authorities to be offensive to the public. The question you posed was, how can an image of a new-born baby offend public taste? I too find this most peculiar. Not having seen this photograph, I wonder if the picture was taken at the moment of birth, when the baby was emerging from its mother's vagina. This is the sort of image that a lot of men, and a lot of women, don't like to see. It makes them feel squeamish. Obviously, a lot of women if photographed in this state would find it deeply offensive for this extremely vulnerable and carnal moment to be seen by anyone, let alone the public. My feeling is that it's not the sexual aspect of the image that people might possibly find upsetting but the powerfully visceral aspect, which brings our fragility and mortality too sharply into focus.

ER: No, the photo by Toscani was not of the mother giving birth, it was just the baby, still covered in blood and mucous, on a white background being held by the obstetrician. Simply a new-born baby. But it wasn't your Pamper's version, it wasn't pink and puffy, it was bloody and viscous. Sure, it was shocking for those who have never seen the birth of a child, or of a baby veal for that matter. Births of mammals are more or less similar. It just goes to show how far we've gone from any kind of relationship with natural processes, like ageing. Who sees wrinkles anymore? Where's the sex content if you're not a full-breasted, ripe young woman? We're mixing up beauty with sex, and life with virtual renderings. It's not what you have or what you show, it's the process. Sex is a process. It's in the process that things are exciting, not in the representation. Today, people get off on *projections*, both interior and exterior—like TV. That's why the art market is booming.

MR: If I might take this a step further, would it be fair to say that most people don't know their own intelligence until they are confronted by it, most likely in the form of a work of art that is designed to make them feel smart? What is put in modern art galleries is about helping the public along culturally. It's mostly an insult. Now that I've seen Toscani's baby, I think the fuss made by the UK authorities is even stupider than I did before I saw the image. Perhaps Tracy Emin should have her baby on the floor of Tate Modern. Is this suggestion in bad taste? Frankly, I don't think Tracy would think this such a dumb idea.

ER: I don't get it when you say that what is put in modern art galleries is about helping the public along culturally. Why is that an insult? I find it a good idea, but I don't see it happening too often. I usually see someone's ego splattered all over the place and the gallery dealer trying to convince the client that *this* artist is certainly the one to watch or that *this* unknown piece by a very famous artist is really quite a find. It's like a treasure hunt with blind people, only the dealer knows where he's taking his client. The clients flatter themselves. They really *feel* when something is right, so they buy on impulse. The more rational ones buy on statistical financial values. Either way, it's a junk bond market. That's why sex is a good seller, who doesn't like sex?

MR: If a work of art excites the libido, the work of art is valuable in a sort of unprecedented way. I tried to find a painting of mine that had been bought by a banker, a really nice guy. I had to find it because someone else with a lot of money wanted to buy it. My banker friend said that he had given it to someone very powerful. He had no choice. Fine, so he gave me the telephone number of this man, who is an international arms dealer. When I telephoned, the man said: "The yellow nude hangs over my bed and I can't tell you how many girls I've fucked with it looking down at me." Oh yes, and he also said: "So, I won't sell it." What could I say?

ER: The libido? We really need to look at the Mother Goddess, at the source, Gaia. It's this concept that attracts everyone to sex. Well, not everyone. Certainly most hetero men, and a certain number of women. It's about our origins, it's about sucking milk, it's about being alive. That's why the Catholic Church was obliged to invent the Virgin Mary, they needed to integrate the Mother Goddess into the faith. Otherwise, they risked losing a lot of voters. I'm not saying this to offend anyone, I have deep respect for anyone's faith, but historically the concept of the Virgin Mary came long after the death of Christ. Sorry if that comes as a surprise, but that's the way it is.[5]

MR: It's interesting that on one hand you have the Virgin Mary and on the other you have Mary Magdalene. Some people believe that Mary Magdalene was the wife of Jesus. Even if she wasn't his wife, she very likely did bring him some comfort sexually. Of course it is a puerile cliché but there is the virgin/whore syndrome to address. When I paint a nude I am very conscious of bringing these two psychological elements into the picture. One appreciates that the woman in the painting is inaccessible, so this makes the tantalisation that much more powerful. It does seem crazy to become excited by an image, but it is what happens. This, I think, is perhaps one of the most magical aspects of imagery, but is it not finally a rather lonely proposition?

ER: If you're talking about being excited by looking at an image while you're alone, yes it is a lonely proposition. But images that excite me are all over the place. Sometimes I'm alone, sometimes not. If sexual images are taken into the flow of dialogue (both visual as well as verbal) that continuously surrounds us, that excitement becomes integrated with our

---

[5] References for the concept of the Virgin Mary:
A History of Western Philosophy, Bertrand Russell, Touchstone, London, 1972, p. 369
The Passion of the Western Mind, Richard Tarnas, Pimlico, London, 1998, p.162
A World Lit Only by Fire, William Manchester, Back Bay Books, New York, 1993, p.12
Inchiesta su Gesù, Corrado Augias & Mauro Pesce, Mondadori, Milan, 2006, p. 90

relationships. These influences might even modify how we relate to one particular person. What I'm trying to say is that the loneliness of male excitement in relation to visual nudity is part of a more complex mechanism. If you chop it up and look at just one part, it *is* very lonely—it is auto-referential, this projective masturbation thing. If, on the other hand, it's part of a more complex dialogue with other people, than it's just that. Visual culture is a very complex reality. It's like communicating on five, perhaps ten levels of Photoshop at the same time. All of the levels are transparent, and the final image—the dialogue—shows all the levels, but each level is a separate entity.

MR: I'm curious to know what you—there in Roman Catholic Milano—know about the myth of Mary Magdalene, a prostitute, being the wife or lover of Christ. I'm most curious because I do believe that this psychological complex must have a lot to do with the way men take a woman's sexuality and use it to heighten their awareness of their own divinity, or should I say *assumed* divinity. Women are often so teasingly vulnerable in photographs that are meant to titillate. It must certainly be a kind of paradox that is being employed psychologically to bring the male viewer to a rewarding conclusion about himself.

ER: It seems that Mary Magdalene was not a whore at all but became one thanks to a much later interpretation of the Bible. About three hundred years after the death of Christ, it was determined, in a rarefied moment of misogynous zeal, that she be elevated to the role of prostitute. Evidently, there is no reference to her being so in the scriptures. The simplistic virgin/whore representation of women has obviously been substantially modified in recent history. It certainly still exists, but it has, like everything else, become a more complex affair. Now women are commanding and self-assertive, neither of which characteristic falls into the virgin/whore categorisation. The misogynous virgin/whore syndrome has a lot to do with other issues, not the least being the influence of Christianity on Western culture. And there are other crucial issues like possession, self-identity, gender-orientation, and personal history. Helmut Newton's images helped change the virgin/whore syndrome, making it into a self-assertive, domineering/whore syndrome. Not an enormous advance, but at least a step into the present. It seems that more women today identify with Newton's perversion than with the previous Catholic one.

MR: The women that are drawn to Helmut Newton's work certainly are trying to find a way through to an assertive state of mind while simultaneously wielding formidable sexual power. The flip side is of course his images of supposedly powerful women disadvantaged by medical braces. Did a man break her neck? we ask. Did she break her arm while doing something exciting? This has a lot to do with Japanese bondage photography. It has a lot to do with the sexual excitation a man might experience when encountering a woman made so helplessly available. I believe the man encountering the bound woman is also helpless: he may take forever to achieve his sexual satisfaction, but he must. My interpretation is that the woman in the photograph is *never* to be touched, and it's this element of tantalisation that the photograph provides.

3.

MR: When you speak of *style* in a photograph, are you referring to our aesthetic response to the photograph as an object or to the self-consciousness of the mind at work behind the photograph? Is style about finding a way to objectify one's sensibility or is it a way of ingratiating one's self with the viewer? In this regard, you mentioned "the overwhelming amount of boring landscape photography which passes for fine art." It occurs to me that landscape photography tends to be so boring because the manifestation of style in the image tends to consume the nature.

ER: When I speak of style, I'm referring simply to both the technical decisions as well as the aesthetic ones, like framing or viewpoint, which each photographer chooses while shooting a photograph. These choices are intrinsically connected with personality and psychology, therefore there are often many constants which make a person's 'style' recognisable. Another thing is the question you mention of the photographer wanting to somehow ingratiate himself to the viewer, or probably more specifically the client. The viewer/client could be the public or a critic, or even a publicly accepted trend. In this way, the photographer is trying to ingratiate himself, but even then sometimes his personal choices are stronger than his will.

MR: I don't often take photographs professionally, so I very rarely have to think about satisfying a client. However since my photographs have begun to appear in art magazines and galleries my perception of them has certainly changed. Naturally, I'm much more conscious of their character—their style—as a kind of totality. I quite often take four and five exposures of the same subject, not to get the light and shadow exactly right, but because I instantly see some aspect of the subject I didn't see in the previous frame. But this must be true of almost anyone who takes a picture. In this way, the subject is much more likely to seduce me when later I appreciate its various aspects as a photograph. When I have to present one particular image to satisfy one particular need, I find it extremely difficult to decide which version of the image to use. I don't have much will power when it comes to using my camera, I'm altogether impulsive—taking photographs from a hotel balcony at four o'clock in the morning, etc. You could say my procedure is self-indulgent in the extreme. But then I step back and ask myself who is going to want to see this, to want to see what I saw at that moment. I often look at a photograph in a magazine and can only think of who exactly it is intended to please, or seduce? The photograph must then be entirely about style.

ER: Well, I don't know if what you're saying is about style or more probably *life-style*—an easy life-style based on narcissism.

MR: Self-image is an addiction. We're now living, especially in cities, amidst swarming masses of spirits addicted to projected images of themselves—projected images of themselves in their minds. Their imaginations are fixed on themselves, on their identity as manifest in their art. In this way, they can be anyone they choose, just as long as they can perfect that image and sell it to someone. How much of it is about finding meaning in the hours that imperceptibly slip by, in the debris in the river? Yes, I have the distinct impression that succeeding at achieving some sort of mythology for one's self is far more important than succeeding at conjuring up an image that truly expresses anything, no matter how obliquely or with what degree of futility. One must have a *strategy* or risk the shame of anonymity.

ER: Here we're opening up a question which touches all contemporary industrialised society: narcissism and self-identity. I don't know how much of this we want to get into just now. So, getting back to the question of urban landscape photography, I find it so intrinsically boring that I can't imagine why anyone would think of doing it. Perhaps the only reason is that it is so easy to do and it appeals to people politically, to people who sponsor projects thinking they're satisfying their need to be culturally involved. Who cares? Since they've missed the boat, I don't think it's worth even thinking about it. As to the manifestation of style tending to consume the nature within the image, I feel more inclined to say that the *total absence* of style is the cause of the boredom. No one really does anything except point the camera.

MR: I'm curious how exactly you would define urban landscape photography as opposed to landscape photography per se.

ER: Industrial sites, city scenes, homes, interiors (that's my liberty, to include interiors in urban landscapes, even though it may seem like stretching the term a bit). I make the distinction because Landscape Photography is also about greenery and the woods and the landscape in general, which isn't really a strong sector, whereas Urban Landscape Photography has filled books, magazines, and museums for decades.

MR: The school of derricks and dereliction. Either we're confronted with humanity's destitution or we're confronted with landscapes so vast that dinosaurs would appear as fleas in their pristine fabric. I can't now recall who said, I like nature outdoors, let's leave it there. I know city-dwellers who live in trembling fear of being subjected to a weekend in the country, especially when their host and hostess are determined *to do something in nature*. Most landscape photographs make me glad I'm not there.

ER: Sometimes the pretty postcard is really quite well done, so I enjoy some pretty postcards. It's your run of the mill amateur masterpiece, but they can be very pleasant to look at. On the other hand, postcards—general landscape photography—can be quite boring because it's *only* descriptive, and doesn't use the visual medium to really say anything. It's the pencil of nature idea—that is, the camera does all the work.

MR: When I was a kid, I used to spend an inordinate amount of time in the woods. The woods were about a fifteen minute walk over the hills from our house. I first went there with my older brother then later, when I wasn't hidden in the basement painting, I would go there on my own to think. Hunsberger's Woods was my sanctuary. My relationship with nature began there, and that relationship was very much an extension of myself. There were extraordinary things to look at, like the murky reservoir shrouded by tall trees, its dark corners patterned in floating leaves, its mesmerising surface occasionally disrupted by the shimmering of a snake. Having had this primordial connection with nature, I've always found it difficult to imagine photographing secret places which I can only consider as sacrosanct. Obviously for others there is an element of discovery to being in nature that excites their image-making instincts. Taking pictures of gardens however is something in which I indulge with great joy. But the garden must be entirely empty and there must be some element of architecture to give the picture shape, to enable me to create a confine against which the most fragile, or luscious, or peculiar aspects of the garden can play.

ER: This brings up an interesting subject, which is the *choice* of subject matter. There's a very early self-portrait that Albrecht Dürer did when he must have been about 23 or something where he is leaning his face on his hand in a very tired way. Now *that* is a breakthrough. Whoever thought in the 1500's that someone leaning on his own hand could be the subject of a drawing! You see that all the time in photography. Someone photographs something which up till that time has been ignored and *voilà*, you've changed the medium and what it says. Like Robert Frank's work in the mid-fifties, like Mapplethorpe's work, or Witkin. They've all shown new subject matter and that has been immensely important for the medium's growth. That's one of the reasons that urban landscape photography is so incredibly boring; it shows us what we already know.

MR: You recently wrote the following about my painting: "I realise that your subject matter is very personal, but I can't help wondering what you might do with contemporary concepts like anxiety, or boredom, or waiting for a bus, or things like that which would give more room for an observer's reflexivity . . . I'm convinced that the key to communicating one's self lies in talking about things that others identify with. I know it's obvious, so very old and obvious, maybe even commercial sounding, but then again, why should anyone look if there's nothing he can grasp? For this reason I'm fascinated by the painting of the man and the peapod vagina. I find it an interesting way to speak about relationships, or about the frustration of a non-relationship."

This I found particularly interesting. But how does one paint an *anxious* still life? I believe it can be done, and it can be done subtly. The man and the "peapod vagina" is an interesting painting for me because I never knew and still don't know what it's about. The title is Lampman, but only because we have a luminous yellow head and neck rising out of a vase (lamp-base) on a table; the "peapod vagina" was originally a leaf that became a kind of orifice due to the painting of the colour around it and the application of short black lines in charcoal along one side of the leaf's long curve. For me, it is an enigmatic image. When you ascribe the "frustration of a non-relationship" to this image, I begin to see what it might be about. It struck me early on that Lampman might be symbolic of latent homosexuality or perhaps an inclination towards trans-sexuality. As you know, I am deeply perplexed by some photographic imagery. This may be because I attribute unintended and diverse meanings to the imagery.

ER: But how could it be any other way! You know, this gets to the heart of a very good point: do you have to know exactly what you're doing in order to do something worthwhile or interesting? That's what's so fascinating sometimes about photography. It reveals new associations, and therefore new trends of thought. Through the mistakes of poor framing, or casual shooting (something contemporary photographers do all the time), diverse elements find their way into the image. We know from gestalt psychology that our eyes do not distinguish between subject and background—only our brains do. We are forced to associate elements which, up until the moment of perception, we have never associated. That, in my opinion, is the revelatory moment, when we make for the first time associations which open up new paths of feeling or thought. As Pirandello said, once you've created the characters, they take on a life of their own.

MR: This is absolutely true. I made this statement in an interview[6] I did with D.A. Blyler: "If I sense the picture is becoming about something, I try to understand what that might be—often by carrying on painting. Suddenly an image might strike me as rather melancholy, or menacing, or, in its diversity of signals, perplexing—it's then that I begin to appreciate the psychology at work in that particular painting, not before. For me, it's essential that the evolution of the image is a mystery, an unfolding mystery, even if the image is something as simple as an empty vase on a table."

As photographers, I wouldn't say that either one of us is much inclined to take on the larger political issues confronting the world. My conviction is that this sort of work is best left to trained professionals, although so-called amateurs often take the best pictures in extreme situations—because they are truly horrified and frightened by what they see. For me, there is a school of photography that relies on painful subject matter to achieve mass recognition, i.e. "Let's go somewhere and

---

[6] Conversation from the Margins, *Displaced Person: Poetry, Pornography & Politics*, Marcus Reichert, Ziggurat Books, London, 2006

photograph the dying and the dead, their charred living-rooms, their fetid bedclothes."

In this regard, I thought you might find a letter I wrote to my friend Roy Oxlade[7] of interest. It's about an article that Martin Amis wrote, published in The Observer, which both Roy and I found perplexing. This, in part, is what I wrote:

"This was not a piece ripe with philosophical illumination, it was essentially a complaint about mankind. Fair enough, but his flippant desperation—if Islam isn't going to go away, why not just surrender to it?—struck precisely the wrong note . . . The subject of religion and its atavistic control of the masses—fundamentalists of all kinds now gone berserk, evangelicals endlessly stating what is morally correct, ladies wandering aimlessly into church yards—is surely one that demands its own arena. So, according to Amis, the current thinking is: to create a secular world in which everyone can do as they please without offending anyone else, it is essential to destroy entire cultures. This, it seems to me, is at the heart of Amis's fascination with the daily apocalypse we are now suffering (or not, if we are clever enough or lucky enough to avoid it)."

If I recall correctly, the photographic image accompanying Amis's article was a high angle of a mass of agitated Arab men. Its use was certainly meant to suggest that the Arab Street, as journalists like to call those mysterious by-ways of Middle Eastern sociology and psychology, is about to devour Western civilisation. This may not have been the photographer's intention whatsoever, the image having been bought from a picture service. I'm curious to know, in terms of making images, how this strikes you.

ER: How does this strike me? Well, it's quite overwhelming. Sure, the distribution of images by picture services makes

[7] Roy Oxlade (1929–) British modernist painter

photographers prostitutes at the mercy of the client's desires. So we get images of depth thrown at us with false captions and misleading explanations. I, unfortunately, have not read Amis's article in The Observer, so I can't comment on that, but the political aspects you speak about—a secular world where anyone should be free to do as he pleases as long as he doesn't harm his neighbour—are the basis of our Western capitalistic society. Nothing new about that. What is missing, in my opinion, is the necessary respect between intellectual effort, ethics, spiritual needs, and personal freedom. I have a good friend who is a brilliant Arab photographer, Samer Mohdad, whose work is a wonderful mixture of reportage and poetry. He always addresses the problems you speak of: images being used to say things they weren't meant to say. It's a very delicate problem and a very serious one. Some day we should have a round table with him about that.

4.

MR: Perhaps you would agree that substance, as it pertains to a comprehensible idea, is the most difficult aspect of an image to perceive and consequently interpret. When I speak of *substance* what I mean primarily is the spiritual block of understanding —profound experience and its anticipated reverberations—that inspires one to make, or capture, a particular image.

ER: Religious iconography is a very good place to begin because it makes obvious the workings of what you call *substance*, or what Erwin Panofsky[8] back in the 40's would have called *intrinsic content*, that is all those elements of symbolism, reference, knowledge, and whatever else one needs to understand—not what one is seeing, but what it all really means. To be quite provocative we could start with a very disturbing image—Serrano's photograph of a crucifix in a bottle of urine. It does bring up a series of conflicting subjects that are pretty relevant today, like carnal reality and iconographic mythology. Or the conflict between what some consider untouchable proof of the Divine and others consider treason. World politics is reflected in the bias of a jar full of piss. It certainly underscores the issue of *substance*.

MR: Serrano's photograph doesn't have very much to do with photography, does it? Really, it was just the most obvious medium in which to get his point across—if one accepts that his point is that religion, specifically Christianity, is worthy of degradation. Serrano takes a complex issue—is religion truly worthy of the dignity it is accorded?—and sensationalises it in good conscience. I don't know if he would be quite so inclined to make such a statement in the Muslim world. Perhaps Serrano was once a Catholic and feels he has the right to make whatever statement he likes using the image of Christ, just as

[8] *Studies in Iconoloty*, Erwin Panofsky, Icon Editions, Westview Press Inc., Boulder, Colorado, 1972

some Jews feel that only they as Jews have the right to criticise Israel. Regardless, the substance of what he is saying with his "piss christ" images is irrefutably that Christian iconography is fair game for non-believers and that so-called blasphemy is inevitable when any religion takes on such smothering characteristics as it does in certain societies. I subjected myself to the wrath of the Christian Right when I chose to exhibit my Crucifixion paintings to benefit the AIDS services of North Carolina. What *right-thinking* Baptist would want his saviour associated with homosexuality and its horrors? Art critics are pretty tame compared to southern preachers who vent their bile on the editorial page of a local newspaper.

ER: In religious images, such as in Serrano's aggressive affront to Christian iconography, there are conflicts involved above and beyond the understanding of *substance* which touch the very fibre of self-identity and its formation. This is where your paintings of the Crucifixion get confused with the moral conduct of homosexuals in the minds of the beholder.

MR: I wouldn't have thought the paintings and their subject were confused with homosexual behaviour in the mind of your average viewer but only in the mind of a Christian viewer predisposed to being offended by Christ's suffering in the context of an exhibition to benefit medical services for dying homosexuals (and anyone else infected with AIDS). Perhaps what you are saying is that the body of Christ, especially as depicted in the act of being crucified, is on some level subliminally about sado-masochism. When a Christian of a certain disposition is confronted with this perverse image essential to his Faith, deep psychological conflict is the intended result.
I would like to stress however that the crucified figure in this series of paintings is not identified as Jesus Christ.

ER: I really don't think that Christ's suffering is subliminally about sado-masochism unless you pin all observation of suffering with some kind of pleasure and I don't think that is true at all. As to not identifying Jesus Christ with the person on the cross in your paintings, that's a fairly ambivalent thing to say in as much as it looks like Christ, so the connection is assured. On the other hand, spiritually speaking, I personally believe that Christ's suffering, like all human suffering, is a general state of affairs, so the subject of suffering is a commonly felt expression.

MR: It's not Christ's suffering that is about sado-masochism, it's the use of such a harrowing image to draw one into the flow of Christian spirituality that is perverse. Without the crucifixion and the resurrection, there would be no dynamic upon which to hang the cult. This image is essential to the Faith. Arguably, all religions that derive from an individual figure were initially cults, until they were given some convincing political form. We can take comfort in Christ's suffering because it puts our own in perspective. My point in not naming the crucified figure was to make the figure more accessible to people suffering without the mythification of Christianity, like someone suffering with cancer, or AIDS, or in any other state of physical degradation. The point is, we must find dignity in our own suffering. For me, the most powerful images of the Crucifixion are the most gruesome. You don't find these anywhere now, you find images of Christ asleep on the cross. I do agree with you that not naming Christ was essentially an impotent gesture. Sister Wendy Beckett[9] and I carried on a long correspondence about this particular dilemma—that is, the painter wanting to express Christ's suffering in good conscience while not being a practising Christian.

ER: I like very much your questioning whether Serrano would have, or even could have, done something like that in the Muslim world. There's nothing worse than having God on your side because it means that the rest of humanity can be done away with. Fairly frightening concept if I ever heard one. By the way, Serrano's photograph is a photograph, so it's got everything to do with photography.

---

[9] Sister Wendy Beckett (1930–), Contemplative Carmelite Nun and Art Critic

MR: For me, it has everything to do with certain techniques applied when taking a photograph to achieve a particular result—it is *conceptual art*, which is, unless I'm very wrong, primarily about documentation.

ER: To visualise a concept is no easy thing, so photographers play with reality and its meaning in order to go beyond it into some other kind of mental space where *ideas* are happening. That's one of the mystifying and exciting things about photography. Here you have this *image* of reality but it doesn't necessarily *represent* reality. In this transition lies the magic.

MR: In Mauro Fiorese's interview with you of 2005, you say: "The cool vision which predominates in contemporary photography, in my opinion, has more to do with our need to keep anxiety at bay than with intrinsic values inherent to photography. I prefer being a bit uncomfortable with myself rather than being coldly cool, and while that leads me to take photographs of sometimes ambiguous meaning, I think that kind of approach allows me to gather material which can also be more revealing. I'm interested in seeing what photography can reveal. I look for those elements which indicate something about relationships. Especially the relationship between ourselves and that sense of identity which floats in our imagination throughout our lives which we call *me*. It's true, I don't want to judge anything, but I do want to discover what my life is about."

This, I think, speaks volumes about just how vulnerable we become when we pursue subject matter that might actually be a statement, no matter how oblique, of our personal philosophy, i.e. one's position with regard to any profoundly engaging aspect of life. This sort of involvement when making images undoubtedly produces a kind of anxiety. We wonder what affect the work will have and, occasionally, dread the consequences, be those consequences rewarding or confounding. So when you say you are interested in what photography can reveal, are you not also saying that you are interested in what photography can reveal about you, because this result would seem inevitable.

ER: I'm convinced that the revelations that photography offers us by stopping time and creating relationships between elements of the real world are at the heart of what visually commands our attention. If you want to take it to an extreme, it's like a mantra. The image is a way of getting in touch with meanings and their consequences for us. As to the anxiety produced by the making, I'm not quite sure I understand that because I really don't feel my work will have any effect on anyone and I'm usually astounded when someone says that it does. It's more something I do to make sense out of the world for me, just as you say. I'm interested in what photography reveals to me, and I have to accept what it inevitably reveals *about* me as well.

MR: So then, one has to ask, why do we photograph the things we do? Very seldom do I have a pre-conceived idea. As you know, this is my approach to painting as well. Usually, I feel compelled to take pictures because I'm in a particular place and will very likely never be in that place again. I behave very much like your average tourist, however I like to go out and take pictures when no else is around, like before dawn until people start going about their daily business. The empty streets concentrate my gaze. Occasionally, I will have glimpsed a particular street or absorbed an exhilarating atmosphere one day that draws me back the next. But I never know what exactly my subject will be when I get there, and even if think I do, it invariably changes.

You recently made the observation that although the human figure seldom appears in my photographs, you nevertheless can feel its presence. If I intend to photograph someone, I do my best to concentrate on that person, but inevitably there is something incidentally inspiring about the moment, like a particular quality of light in the room or even a piece of furniture. I very seldom think about what the image might mean,

I only act intuitively on what I somehow recognise as meaningful—meaningful in its peculiar beauty. I find your work engaging as it pertains to the flow of humanity. And I often feel that your subject has been caught unawares, and that is not to say that your camera is at all predatory, as is the case with some photographers. If there is meaning in your images, for me it is predominately enigmatic.

ER: Well, my images are definitely low-key, and I don't mean in a Zen way at all. That's the point for me. But starting with your comments on taking photographs, you simply have not, or do not wish to, accept the responsibility of choosing a theme or subject matter for fear of destroying the spontaneous aesthetic which you (and I) so dearly embrace. But it is a choice on our part. You rely on your wits and your instinctive aesthetic which has always brought you exciting results. But there are worlds of other ways to photograph and we see that all over.

I've got nothing against taking pictures without any preconceived idea, but editing and being sensitive to the image after it's taken is the same thing as thinking heavily before taking the photo. The process changes in its order but the equation remains the same. You don't show just any old image, there's always one that seems to capture better than others the things you feel you have expressed. The only real difference is that the theme or idea expressed is revealed to you through the image-taking process instead of it being generated by some other thought process.

So what's the difference? You might say the spontaneity. I would add the depth of the revelation which for me is always more interesting, and certainly surprising, when captured spontaneously rather than most subject matter produced by my own thought process. But this is not always the case and most contemporary photography attests to that. It is much more about preconceived ideas, in the sense of programmed subject matter, than about spontaneity. There's another aspect to spontaneity which, I believe, is the spiritual: being part of the whole. It’s reassuring to allow life to flow through you and reveal itself through your images. It gives you time to wonder.

5.

MR: You suggested that we talk about the transition from portraits of people to portraits of ourselves, and I assume what you mean by this is the way in which images of people have become more subjective. Basically, we now impose our own psychology on the person we are photographing and it's through this dimension of interpretation that we communicate the character of the person being photographed. It's a form of prejudice and—here I return to one of your most plangent considerations—narcissism. You've said that the photographer often is fulfilling a need of the society he lives in to photograph people as the society sees itself. This is rather complex, but I think I know what you're getting at.

When, in so many words, you refer to an evolution of imagery that embraces, historically, August Sander, Paul Strand, Richard Avedon, Diane Arbus, Cindy Sherman, and Pierre & Gilles, my head begins to swim. Apparently, the images these photographers created were *right* for their time, but neither one of us, I think, is at all certain that portraiture *per se* is what they were about. David Douglas Duncan was very good at capturing the spirit and atmosphere of what Pablo Picasso was about. We have a better understanding of Picasso's life and his relationship to his environment, including the people and animals with whom he was intimate, because of the photographer's rapport with his subject. These are not narcissistic images, neither for the photographer nor his subject. In some cases, there is a kind of *faux* grandeur to the image which obviously the photographer and his subject found amusing when the picture was being taken. David Douglas Duncan is not exploiting his subject, not as, let's say, Diane Arbus might have exploited her subjects. Then of course you have the confrontational aspect of Richard Avedon's work.

It's interesting to contemplate the victimisation of a *voracious* celebrity, i.e. using someone who craves attention, and will do just about anything to get it, for one's own purposes. How best to make a despised political figure look a fool? This, as we know, isn't very difficult, so powerful people rely contractually on the *right of approval*. People who aren't at all powerful, people who haven't the slightest idea what the photographer is about, simply acquiesce.

ER: Aren't *all* portraits an exploitation of the subject? Duncan's photos of Picasso weren't portraits but a visual narrative. They don't exploit the subject. But anyone who has tried seriously to work with portraiture realises that the subject is manipulated by the photographer, and by the photograph, and there isn't much you can do about that, it's a visual consequence. So, one thing is taking responsibility, the other is exploiting the individual for your own or someone else's needs. Diane Arbus, quite honestly, exploited her subjects in her own desperate quest for a sense of identity. Avedon, on the other hand, is admittedly manipulative, but in order to use the human canvas to talk about humanity. Not necessarily the *subject's* humanity, but humanity itself.

MR: I now feel compelled to talk about *lookism*, which I find particularly nasty. They perfected this form of prejudice in America, and now the entire world practices it to some degree. Although it isn't about racial purity, one's face must conform to a standard, otherwise one is excluded. If you don't conform and want to be a success at what you do, best to do your correspondence by e-mail rather than have a meeting. A symmetrical face is a face worth having, and worth knowing. Lookism is a strain of social pathology that apparently has been developing for a fairly long time. The perfect example is what I would call *the lost child* syndrome. Why do news programmers make a big fuss about a *beautiful* child who goes missing, showing her image again and again, and show no concern whatsoever for a child in the same distressing situation who isn't, by the usual standards, very pretty? This is deplorable, but it is what has become of the dominating societies of Western civilisation. Rape and other extreme forms of humiliation can conversely also be a result of lookism.

And the flip-side is of course a fascination with the grotesque. But, getting back to the prejudicial nature of *the lost child* syndrome, I would say that finding beauty *and* dignity in humanity, whether dressed for a funeral or undressed for a fling in the pool, is now first and foremost about *phoney idealism*. I'm talking about the Ralph Lauren school of thought. I see idealism in this *perverted* form as a deluding and ultimately degrading influence on humanity. I regret that this sounds so terribly grand in its pessimism. When it comes down to it, dealing with this sort of idealism can be infuriating, because the people who endorse and practice it are so implacably correct in their attitude, especially in their relations with unlike people—that is, people who they consider beneath them socially for any number of reasons. Anyone with any good sense must realise how horrifying all of this is.

ER: It's really about the farce of the good life, the American way, etc. It's *Disneyland*. People want to believe that everything is pristine and perfect, which boils down to simple hypocrisy. Nice little girls with golden curls. Very Puritan, very unreal. This is the first I've heard of *lookism*, but I've always felt that the publishing of images of missing children on all our tax returns and milk cartons and the like was a public service as well as the sign of a sick society, a society that has lost its capacity to care for children. You also referred to the *grotesque* which I find more interesting. I think people are attracted to the grotesque because they are curious to see someone who's worse off than themselves. It's a pathetic kind of pat on the back. "I'm OK, look at this creep" kind of thing. But the grotesque is also a way of injecting emotion into a bland environment. We live in a floating world of perfect women, perfect faces, and perfect happiness—according to the consumer philosophy—so the punk spirit of spitting in someone's face activates a kind of perverse pleasure. We are touching something real for a change, but it's a desperate attempt at feeling *normal* ourselves.

MR: The desperation is interesting, both in Arbus's approach and in our response to her images. This is somewhat off the subject, but once I've taken in the figures and faces in her photographs, I then look around the scene, be it a room in someone's house or a public park. Sometimes the circumstances in which her subjects live tell me more than the subjects' faces, or the expressions on their faces. This is where an Arbus photograph works for me, and I wouldn't say her choice of setting is at all incidental.

ER: Those surroundings are the bits and pieces of reality that just happen to be in the frame when the photograph is taken. That's what I love about casual framing, it throws unwanted things into your image. Then when you look at the photograph, you're forced to make sense of all these bits and pieces, which is often very revealing.

MR: You may recall the importance of National Geographic Magazine when we were kids—I believe this periodical is still a thriving success. A large part of its ability to fascinate had to do with images of *exotic* peoples. You never knew who you were going to find beautifully photographed in their natural habitat. One issue it might be New Guinea tribesmen, the next Mongolian villagers. They all appeared to quite love having their pictures taken. But not everyone felt this way. Somewhere along the line, I learned that certain Eskimo tribes refused to have their pictures taken because they believed that by being photographed their souls were captured and kept. They believed that the person who then held the image of them had robbed them of their spirit and consequently controlled their destiny. When considering celebrity in the image-obsessed world we live in, this superstition would seem less a superstition and more a reality. It's often the subject's notoriety that becomes the reality. His life becomes unreal and sometimes falls apart altogether.

ER: Here we go back to the question of *reflexivity*. Both the National Geographic photo—the *good* explorer and *good* colonialism—and images of Hollywood Stars reveal society's view of the individual. Within every photograph of a Star is the latent hope that someday you will be loved by someone like that, or you will have the perfection of someone like that.

MR: As a teenager, I used lie in my bed with a photograph of a naked, or semi-naked woman that I was particularly entranced by and wonder as I masturbated if I should concentrate my gaze on her body or her face. Naturally, my eyes roved over her entire image, but I found at the end that I was invariably transfixed by her face. If I were writing a bad song, I would say that I found myself falling into her, or my idea of her, through her face as printed on the page of the magazine. When I was older, I took the photographs myself.

ER: On a semiotic level, you can see how visual elements become synonymous with our desires, or the other way around, with our fears. That's why visual culture is so important. Most people simply don't have the slightest clue as to why they like some images and detest others. Visual ignorance. The world is full of it.

MR: Yes, and what we fear is often also what we desire. But is what we desire ever what we fear? If it isn't perhaps it should be. For too many people, the heart beats faster with the anticipation of war—this was especially true of the invasion of Iraq, and anyone who denies it is, to put it crudely, either deluded or a liar. Following on from there, are there any images that you find repellent or, more specifically obscene, or do you maintain complete democracy of vision?

ER: No, there are plenty of images which I consider really disgusting or immoral and which I try to avoid seeing. People jumping from the World Trade Center is certainly high on my list. I refuse to look at the television when they run that stuff. Any war image of people blown apart to me is disgusting—I just turn away. I don't think sexual pornography is particularly immoral or disgusting, it's just pretty phoney and sometimes silly. It's exciting for about a thirtieth of a second, then you ask yourself what these people were really doing when they posed for the pictures. I often tell my students that a perfect postcard of a sunset is really a pornographic image because, like pornography, it's the maximum visual exploitation with minimum emotion, or no emotion at all. Once you take emotion away from experience, you've got pornography. War imagery is highly pornographic.

MR: You may find it pornographic but it's all we have to communicate the reality of man's barbarism.

ER: But it can't substitute for experience. The problem isn't the message but what it does to our sense of reality. We are out of touch with *real* reality, as opposed to a represented one. Our lives are becoming *completely* contextualised by a *representation* of reality. Look at this image we're told, *this* is what you should be reacting to, *this* is what you should use to make your judgements. But if we haven't lived the experience, how can we know who the good guys are and who the bad guys are?

MR: You are undoubtedly aware that military personnel in America are now almost exclusively professional. In other words, they're mercenaries. If they attach themselves to the right area of expertise, their job is to kill, and to be killed. Obviously, in war you can't have the one without the other. Frankly, these guys have a lot of fun. They even look funny in their big puffy outfits, like post-apocalyptic clowns. Sometimes they protect people from other people and sometimes they just, according to their orders, wreck people's lives. It really doesn't make much difference, because they're being paid to do a job and they *are* professionals. But when one of *our* boys gets killed in action it's a tragedy. The mom and dad sitting at home who encouraged the young lad to be brave are now very upset. Junior is now irreplaceable. Bear in mind though, it was pretty exciting while it lasted. The good news is that now mom and dad get to have a hero for a son. As Lance Corporal Banks said to himself as he realised his face was now in shreds decorating the bougainvillaea: *Wow, this is for real!* But this is just what Americans don't get to see on *reality* TV.

ER: What do reality shows and the like do for our personal relationships? I think they ruin them, I think people are not developing the skills for living and making decisions because they have been denied *real* experience. So you don't know what's real and what's fantasy and you end up believing that you are the good guy and all the others are the bad guys. It's called paranoia, and I think that much of our *represented* reality encourages an emotional detachment usually associated with schizophrenia and paranoia. I'm not saying everyone is quite so emotionally detached, but the *illusions* which are being taken for granted contribute to this kind of mental breakdown. Breakdown in the sense of breaking down mental structures which serve to sustain our concept of reality and the reality in our lives. Destroy that, muddle the distinction between real and unreal, take away emotional experience and substitute it with images which don't have any odour, or natural sound, or physical presence, and I think you end up with a very shaky idea of what your life is about. A beautiful sunset is often no longer rewarding because it *doesn't* have saturated colours or deep blacks. Digital photography does. But what does the *simulacro* do to your mind?

MR: Stephen Barber[10] refers often in his writing to digital screens, be the setting Tokyo or Los Angeles. In his writing, digital screens are everywhere. Initially, I thought Stephen had conjured up this omnipresent element as a kind of ghostly reminder of what the future holds for those of us who live in cities, but then I realised that his digital screens were everywhere already. I'm staring at one right now and this evening I'll be staring at another.

---

[10] *The Vanishing Map*, Stephen Barber, Berg, Oxford & New York, 2006

ER: Images used to give us information, pleasure, and poetry. Today they often numb us and create illusions, especially digital imagery which is *only* illusion. Now I'm not saying this because I want to go back to the past, I only ask myself in what way can I better the situation. I personally believe by teaching, which is what I do. I try to give people the *tools* to help them decipher what's happening. That's why I believe in some of my images. That's why I enjoy your paintings: they give me things to think about in a refreshing way. Sometimes your work is laden with darkness, but usually even this is presented in almost candy-like colour. Your love of colour betrays whatever anxiety lies underneath.

MR: You're the first person I've heard refer to my colour in this way. Perhaps the paintings I was making when we first met, those pictures inspired most by Arshile Gorky, had a kind of synthetic colour to them, but then they had titles like *Cancer Blossom*.

ER: Obviously, you don't use *candy colours*, but I was looking for a word that expressed the rich saturation of colour I find in some of your paintings. Of course I haven't seen everything you've done, but I've seen everything of yours printed in books, and I've re-seen some of that work in your home. The reference to anxiety is connected to both the themes you use, and have used, in your work, and your use of weighty black lines to describe a person or a face. This gestural use of black sometimes gives a kind of weight to the figure itself. A kind of darkish seriousness against a very vivacious background. There's a lot happening.

MR: This brings us full-circle, back to the face, back to portraiture. The few portraits I've painted in my life have nearly all been *inadvertent*. What I mean by that is that the image of a particular person just emerges as I'm painting, or there may be a head in the finished picture which is undeniably someone. Now I know who you are, I'll say to myself eventually, you're the woman I passed on the square that snowy night in Zagreb. And it is.

ER: I think in the end, all portraiture is somewhat about ourselves or a part of ourselves. My images for the *What's wrong?* series, which started out as simply *Tired Women*, is all about my mother and her exhaustion. When we photograph someone else, inevitably we react to that part of the person we recognise and use it to convey our sense of that person to others. It's like making love to strangers in a very intimate way.

MR: This is what politicians are about, isn't it? It's what journalists call the *Elvis factor*. As the one making the portrait, you must inhabit some part of your subject's psychology, no matter how minuscule, tangential, fragile, or perverse that secret relationship might be. I find photographing people in the portrait mode altogether exhausting. But, as you know, it can be hugely satisfying, and you get to know your subject—to an unexpected extent—in the process. Piers Faccini[11] and I decided to work together, to create images of him that we both would find interesting. I know we learned a lot about each other, and now we talk about our work and our lives very openly. This can happen, and it's marvellous.

[11] Piers Faccini (1970–), British/Italian singer, songwriter, and painter

6.

MR: You suggested that we talk about Jean-Michel Basquiat and Jeff Wall. I knew Basquiat, but I didn't know anything about Jeff Wall until I researched his work on the internet. I can't say I can get a grip on Wall's work at all, so why don't we begin with Basquiat.

I first knew of Jean-Michel before I actually met him—I saw SAMO's (Basquiat's pseudonym) graffiti around Soho. I was engaged by it. Jim Galate photographed me on a downtown street early one morning being embraced by a drunken derelict guy as Jean-Michel spray-painted a wall behind us. It was embarrassing, and I hate graffiti, but I admired Jean-Michel. I got to know him at the Mudd Club, where we used to dance together, neither one of us being attached to any one girl at the time. He wasn't like a black American at all. He was like a European African stranded in America. He knew he had to play the game, but he was only going to do it on his terms.

Jean-Michel's painting was altogether disrespectful of the New York Art that had gone immediately before, as was Julian Schnabel's. There was a school of thought at the time, of which I was a member, that said: Fuck elegance, poetry is elegance enough. Any good poetry is initially inscrutably beautiful—it makes you stop and wonder. Jean-Michel knew this. Forget all the rubbish about bringing hip-hop into painting, Jean-Michel was about subjugating art magazine elitism. We were sick to death of Robert Ryman and Richard Serra. Jean-Michel's references to people like Charlie Parker had essentially to do with isolation. When you make *real* outsider art, you *are* an outsider But the painting had to be beautiful, and Jean-Michel knew it—it had to be beautiful with a disarming innocence. For me, it's this innocence that should never be lost, that should always be the approach to painting. Now that everyone knows about these things, it's even more difficult to maintain one's innocence. Jean-Michel succeeded.

ER: Well, I'm a late comer to Basquiat and nothing, I feel, could be farther from Jeff Wall's images. I didn't meet or know Basquiat, neither do I know Jeff Wall. I simply look at their images and their work. Basquiat's is full of refreshing innocence, smart rebellion, and a sharp eye for textures, colours, and graphics. Wall's work is contemplative, abstract, and very demanding of the viewer. Basquiat gives the viewer a pinball machine version of life and Wall asks the viewer to think about what he sees, contemplate its meaning, and understand its references. Wall is a very erudite photographer. On the more personal side, it's easier to appreciate Basquiat because it's easier to play with his visual elements. Wall often appears enigmatic, when not simply boring. As you insinuate, that says a lot about the art world.

MR: Perhaps a lot of this has to do with one's own acute sense of discrimination. I find most of Wall's work to be "simply boring." But then, I find a lot of photography simply boring. I'm not very good at penetrating certain enigmas, especially when I can't *find* the enigma—because I can't find any mystery in the work. What's particularly interesting for me when comparing these two artists, which may be a ridiculous idea in the first place, is the manifestation, or lack thereof, of joy in their work. I find many of Wall's images totally lacking in exuberance. One can't deny Basquiat's exuberance. Do Basquiat's paintings make me happy, like, let's say, a vase of luscious summer flowers? I'd have to say *yes*, sometimes they do. Would a Jeff Wall photograph of a vase of luscious summer flowers make me equally happy? I doubt it. My point is that a Basquiat painting doesn't have to be about anything to excite me. When a photographer like Wall attempts to make some sort of a statement, no matter how perfectly he executes the image, I too often find myself alienated by his aesthetic. I imagine some people find Basquiat's aesthetic alienating too.

ER: I agree with pretty much all you say. I'd find it hard to believe that someone could find Basquiat's aesthetic alienating. It's simply too full of energy and visual joy. Wall, on the other hand, is part of a very serious art market which thrives on *provoking thought*. I'm not excited by Wall's work, but that's not the point. Photography is a language and anyone can say what he wishes. In our written language, you can write a poem or a laundry list, so why shouldn't photographers and other artists say such different things? Wall doesn't have to be joyful for us, he can be intellectually perverted. Who cares? What bothers us, I think, is that he makes a lot of money doing it, but that, I believe, has more to do with his business tactics as an artist than simply the thoughts behind his work.

MR: It's difficult for me to grasp how Wall makes any money with his photographs, but then I'm very much outside the art magazine culture that spawns such fantasies about the meaningfulness of art. I believe that if there is any meaning in any work of art it is necessarily elusive. I'm not at all certain that the mind is actually capable of ascertaining meaning unless it is in the service of a scientific equation. For me, the beauty of meaning is its meaninglessness, its relevance being our need to find meaning. Perhaps what I'm saying is that the meaning is in the experience of the thing. I believe we are now steadfastly drifting away from any comprehensible form of reality. Our acts become increasingly meaningless as we witness the actions of the most powerful among us.

I find Damien Hirst's art amoral, although he might claim that he is making some sort of a statement about the hollowness of contemporary values. Actually, knowing his work, I can appreciate that this might be a worthwhile view for him to have, but I still find most of what he does grossly synthetic. Why make art that is perfectly manufactured when in a nano second it is merely another manufactured wonder? If it were mine to have, I would trade his diamond-encrusted human skull for something more profoundly ephemeral, like a real tear-jerking story of woe, any day. Where does our empathy kick in and our wonder retreat into the dark shadows of our own gluttony? When do our appetites ever serve the needs of someone else, especially when our appetites have been abstracted by someone else's self-indulgent aesthetics? For me, the enigma becomes a kind of damnation. As long as we keep it vague and filled with possibility, there is no relief.

ER: You seem to be alluding to an emptiness, a human emptiness, in contemporary art and society. OK, we all know there is a big game going on between young artists, critics, and the public. The game is called: Who's one step ahead? Where's the cutting edge? Is it enough to be clever and leave everyone lying in the dust, gasping for breath? I think this is what you're saying, that it's not. Cool, smooth surfaces are part of the modern ethic, especially when surfaces become the most important part of a being. *Surfaces* means superficial. Speed up time, don't give anyone a chance to catch a breath. In the end you're in a kind of side-show at the circus where you have two seconds to capture the passer-by. That's when cleverness becomes important. But in a secular society, where the overriding values are profit, money, and speed, you don't get a chance to recapture any value that takes more than two seconds to be understood. You can't *live* experience while zapping through your life. So artists play the art game. They dazzle for a second, just long enough to be solidified by a speculative market in need of a fix.

MR: I like what you say about *smooth surfaces*. Basquiat's surfaces were not smooth. His life was not smooth, and he lost himself to heroin. When you speak of the warmth lacking in humanity, and why that lack exists, I think of the inexplicable warmth in Basquiat's painting, and this warmth existed *in spite of* the fact that he too was playing the art game. I'm very much looking forward to our discussion on painting and religion, because it is the spirituality in painting that I find most moving. If one finds the word *spirituality* off-putting, it might be helpful to elaborate on the simplicity of this concept as it relates to an activity like painting. And in this regard, there are other words that have a similar resonance, like illumination, revelation, discovery. When in the midst of these sensations, things suddenly become quite simple—they become clear, and if they aren't clear, and we acknowledge this to ourselves, these same sensations lead us on to discover more about what we are doing. This is art that is not wholly pre-conceived and immaculately executed, it is art that is often ill-conceived and miraculously salvaged.

There is so much that you've just said that I find absolutely true. For instance, I think we all suffer from our own apathy. Apathy is inevitable, but inertia certainly isn't helpful when it comes to making slick art. Perhaps you would agree that the rough edges, rather than the cutting edges, often give an image, be it a painting or a photograph, its depth. The rough edges insure that the image will remain interesting, perhaps even a bit inscrutable. I do believe that Jeff Wall knows this, I'm just not at all certain that it comes to him naturally. In his defence, I don't believe that the rough edges in Francis Bacon's work came to him naturally—not in the world of subservience to style in which he developed—and that he had to work very hard to lose himself in what the paint could accomplish without an enormous amount of premeditation. It may be the premeditation that I see in so much art that leaves me cold.

7.

MR: Today, I have a fairly typical problem. I have a painting that I've been working on over the past several weeks, one which I assumed a few days ago was finished. But, as often happens, now I'm not convinced that the painting is what it truly wants to be. In this case, it has primarily to do with colour. The painting has emerged through five states of transformation. On one side of the canvas is a tall bluish pink vase on a pedestal against a background of mottled colour predominated by a kind of dusty raw sienna; on the other side is a vertical mass of gestures, again in raw sienna but over some scribbled writing in ink, smears of orange, and a wash of milky white like an old limestone wall. When I imposed the pink vase on the painting, everything changed, but I wasn't completely aware of just how it had changed. Now I feel I need another colour, perhaps a green of some sort, overlaying the vertical mass of gestures across from the pink vase on its pedestal.

I approach the problem of colour when taking a picture in much the same way I do when making a painting: I restrict my use of colour as much as possible until I can find some psychological resonance in the colour that is then allowed into the image. When taking a photograph, this is a tricky proposition because it tends to make the image look designed, even though the image existed in its totality before I invaded the scene. For me, it is this *psychology of colour* that enables the image to communicate on a subliminal level. Augmented by light and darkness, the colour encourages us to partake of an alien reality, which is in reality what the photographer sees.

Unless we art direct our photographs, which of course is not uncommon, we are obliged to make something of the colour that presents itself naturally in our frame—we must use our *selective* instincts to realise the colour of a compelling image. Obviously, colour can be used in innumerable ways. It can be used violently or very subtly, so subtly that the image might initially appear to be monochromatic. Colour is a big problem in many photographs. Because there isn't a discriminating eye at work behind the camera, the image is a hodgepodge of colour, or it has a random and banal kind of colour that enforces itself (occasionally intentionally) on the viewer. It's as if we are being subjected to the dictates of a school of *non-colour*.

ER: Yes, but a photographer *can* work with colour in many ways, especially today with digital technology. Whereas once you really had to take what the film gave you, today you can do pretty much as you like with colour. It's just that few people actually intervene because it's easier to let the machines do the work. However, since you can manipulate all colours, reality is no longer a bind for the photographer. My relation to colour has been a strong constant in my life and has affected immensely both my personal as well as professional life. I built my career professionally on using colour where others hadn't.

MR: Your colour is often startling. And I feel very strongly that what you might call your 'commercial' work is fine art by the standards of anyone who appreciates those qualities that confirm the poetry of an image. There is an undeniable dimension of colour being used for purely aesthetic reasons in your 'commercial' work. Because of this, much of your industrial work pre-figured the current school of what I would call 'factory' photography. Marco Torres, a friend of mine in Marseilles, recently discovered the potential for documenting arresting colour in defunct industrial buildings. He produced an entire suite of images from one site, much as you would fulfil a commercial contract. But, as I said before, when you fulfil a commercial contract you are in essence producing a suite of poetical images.

For me, there are various ways to achieve some psychological impact with the photographic images I make. I have found one film stock that works extremely well for me: the ancient and wholly reliable Kodachrome 64. But the most important element for me in this process is light and shadow—that is, light and shadow as opposed to light and dark. The value and depth of any colour that enters my frame is of course taken into account, but light and shadow really tend to fasten me to a scene or subject. This of course carries over into my film work, most particularly when I have to work with what is in front of me, rather than what colour I might apply to the scene.

Everyone talks about the colour in the film *Union City*, and I went to enormous lengths to create an atmosphere of claustrophobia with the colour I imposed on my interiors. What was not only interesting but a kind of revelation for me were the images Amos Chan, our stills photographer, got in those rooms. Because he wasn't concerned with the drama, his images have an objectivity that for me is absolutely fascinating. But not only did he *objectify* my colours, he also brought a completely different psychological resonance to them—he used them to express the tension (and its release) inherent to making a dramatic film. My feeling is that this sort of transformation of a scene can be achieved anywhere if we intuitively know what sort of a response we are hoping to provoke.

ER: It's interesting that you accept the *change* that Amos Chan's photographs wrought on your original use of colour. Usually people are dissatisfied with someone who changes what they believe to have been their original idea. But the attention one gives to the transition from light to shadow is certainly an interesting part of the spectrum because it's the least visible, and it's where colours loose their saturation and tend towards grey. It deepens the senses—you're on the verge of loosing your visual capabilities, and you get lost in the shadows, both literally and metaphysically.

As to your choosing a film like Kodachrome 64, thanks for the nostalgia. Kodachrome doesn't exist any longer in Italy and so it's simply a memory. One can change films to find some kind of interesting colour, but one can't change the chemical process in order to modify anything, one can only filter the scene to modify the colour while shooting. At any rate, that's the past for most of us. Today, we work in a digital environment where the meaning of *colour* has been greatly enlarged and put directly into the hands of the artist or photographer. We no longer depend solely on the manufacturer or his chemical processes. Sure, we depend on the pigments in the inks, but our ability to modify the tone, hue, saturation, contrast, and intensity of each and every pixel opens up a new world of expression which we have only just begun to explore.

MR: Actually, Kodachrome 64 can still be bought in Europe. It is processed exclusively at the Kodak lab in Switzerland. It's what I use almost exclusively. Naturally, because this is transparency film scanning is necessary before printing. The scans can be modified as you suggest to achieve myriad variations in the image. My inclination with my work for galleries and collectors is to modify the image as little as possible. Having said that, I always provide my printer with guide prints that I make on my Hewlett Packard Deskjet 840C, which is just about the least sophisticated printer you can buy, however the results for my purposes are absolutely fine. I have only just begun to work with a digital camera, but that has been primarily to document paintings, or perhaps to grab a few pictures of the garden to send in jpg to someone like yourself.

ER: It's very nice of you to mention my industrial work. I am very fond of my professional work and I'm glad you can see how I always tried to 'produce a suite of poetical images'. Very few people would tend to agree with you about that. To most, my work is simply a commercial application of photography with saturated colours in places where saturated colours were hard to find. I always felt greatly misunderstood on that point because for me my images *were* a suite of poetical images. They just happened to narrate things the client was interested in showing. I love their formality, deep colours and poetry. I've always been fascinated looking into industrial reality. I always found it rich in meaning and human presence. Thousands, millions of people working on the smallest of problems just to make some package slide better on a conveyor-belt or to render some die-cutting monster a little safer. All industrial processes are fascinating and I always tried to visualise the majesty and beauty of these machines, hidden in some dark corner of an industrial foundry or in the middle of an enormous industrial site. But since I never dealt with the common themes of the day, such as the politics of the industrial world and its workers, or even the sort of aloof documentation of the Bechers,[12] I've found only a very small audience who appreciate my work as personal expression.

MR: Your taste for saturated colours electrifies your images. In conjunction with your composition, which I've always found to be impeccably realised, the effect is sensational. And form truly comes alive. In some of your images the atmosphere is almost intimidating, if not a trifle ominous. I would love to see an entire book of your industrial work. Again, my colour tends to hinge on light and shadow. For me, black is a colour, whereas for others it is an idea, like *white* is an idea. If we make the effort to look into the shadows, into what might superficially appear to be merely an area of deep shadow, we see colour, and often colour of astounding variety. I've found pockets of shadow that are violet, that glow. When the lower regions of a street are drenched in shadow, the buildings rising out of that shadow take on a grandeur unknown in sunlight alone.

ER: For me, colours are rich feelings which soak the object and leave us emotionally satisfied. It's like music, the melody is fundamental, but if there isn't any rhythm it's just noise, and if there isn't any silence, again it becomes just noise. Colour is like that: its abundance is emotional, but only if there is some kind of visual order, and a limit to the quantity of colour. Otherwise, it's just garish, disgusting overstimulation with little or no emotional impact. As with everything, the mixing of elements tends to enrich the experience while the overuse

---

[12] Hilla Becher (1934–) & Bernd Becher (1931–), German photographers and teachers

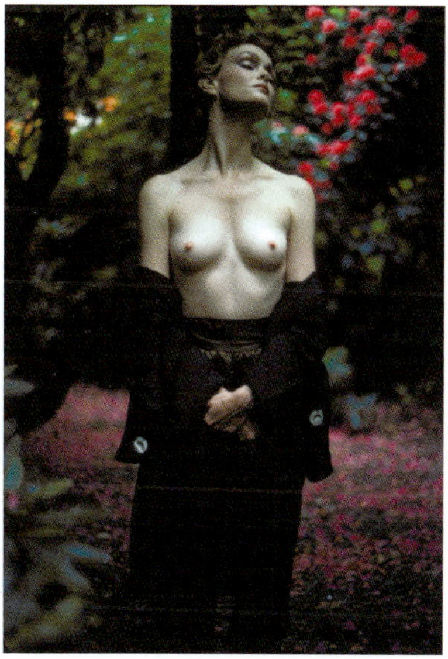

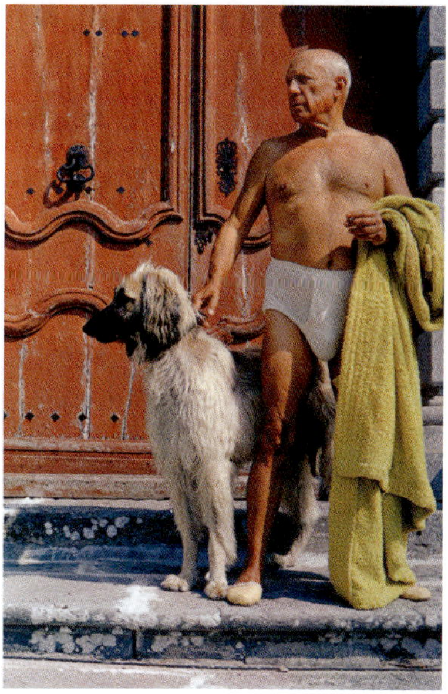

Marcus Reichert, *Sally MacLeod, London,* 1979
David Douglas Duncan, *Pablo Picasso, Mougins,* 1962

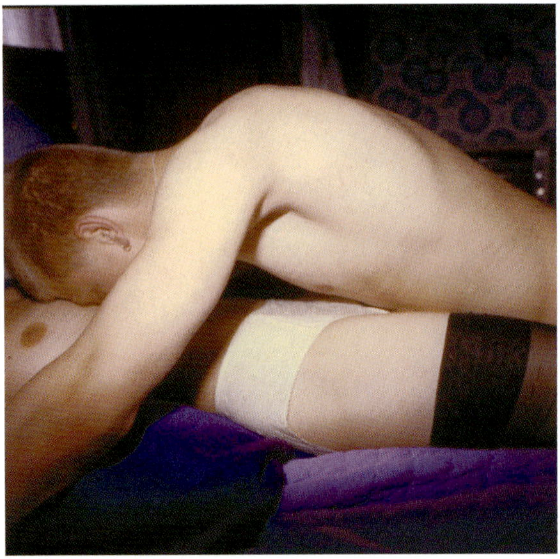

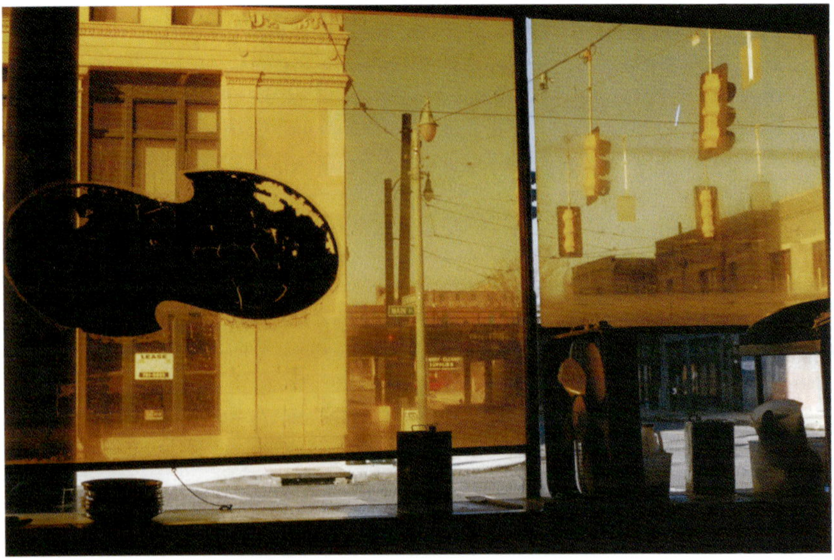

Nan Goldin, *Skinhead having sex, London,* 1978
William Eggleston, *Untitled (Memphis, Tennessee)*, 2000

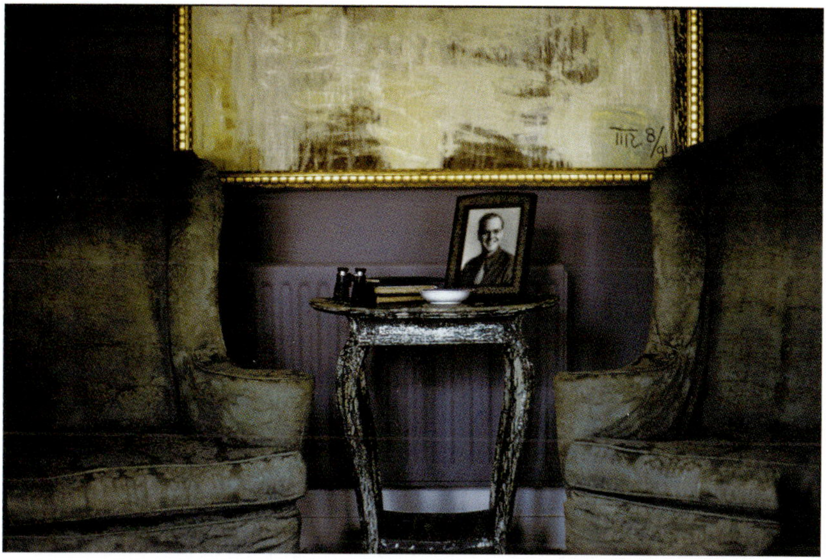

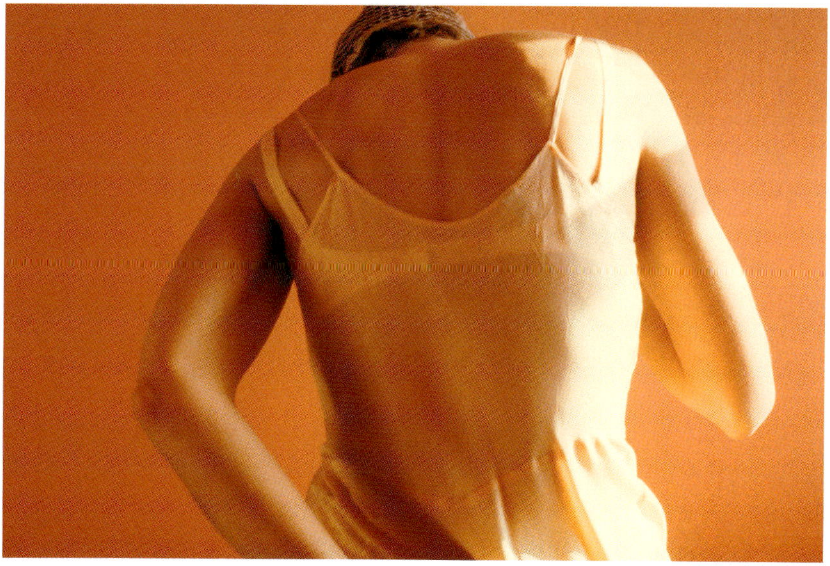

Marcus Reichert, *Drawing-room, Ramsgate,* 2002
Amos Chan, *Union City* (production still), 1979

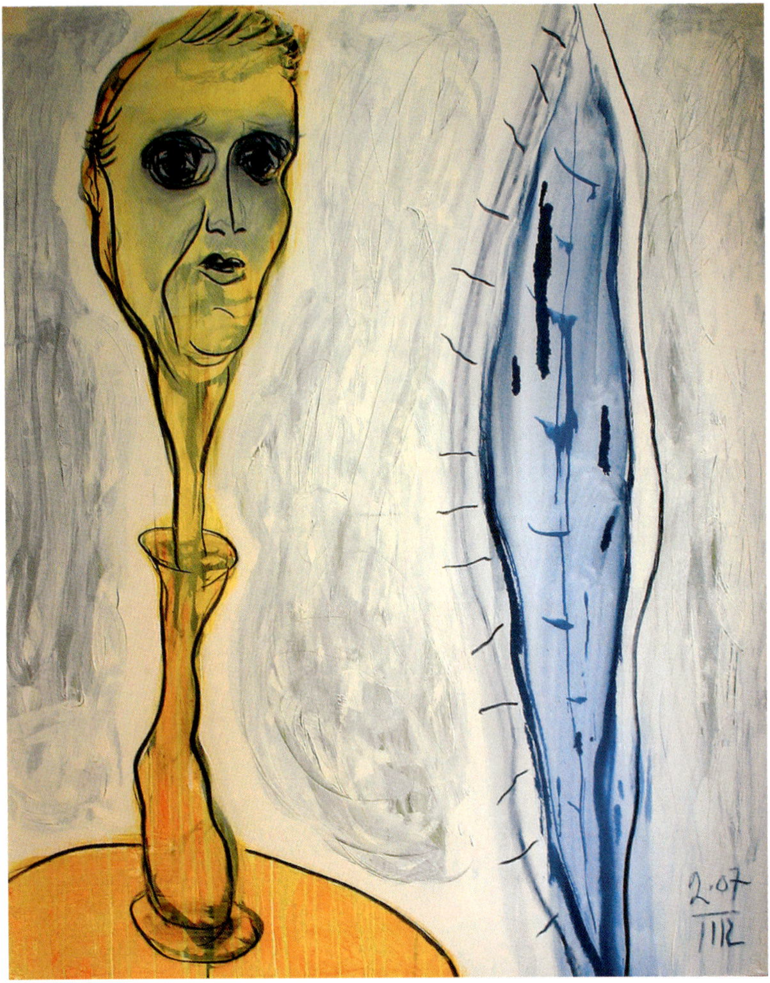

Marcus Reichert *Lampman,* 2007

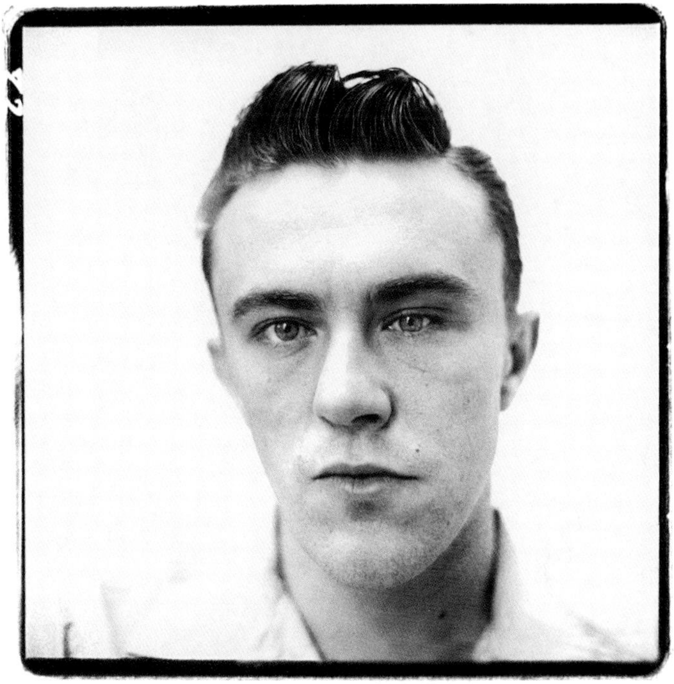

Richard Avedon, *Dick Hickock, murderer, Garden City, Kansas, April 15, 1960*

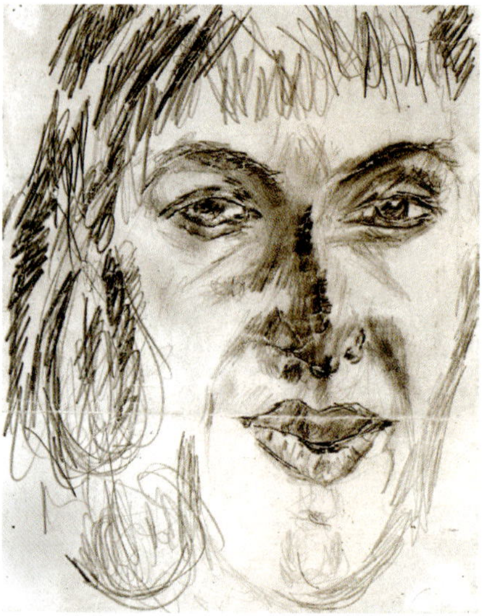

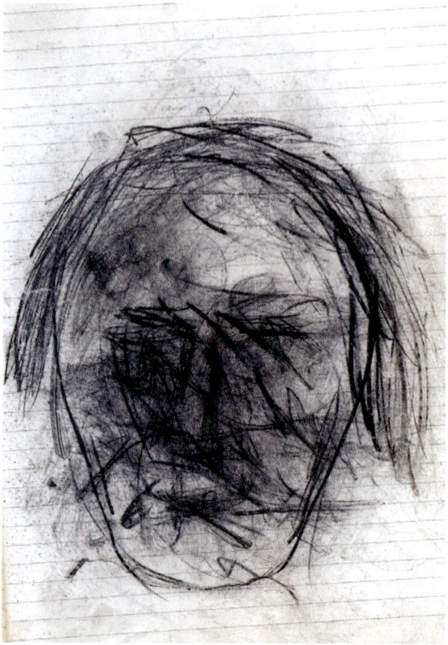

Antonin Artaud, *Portrait of Mania Oïfer*, 1947
Piers Faccini, *Head of Antonin Artaud*, 1990

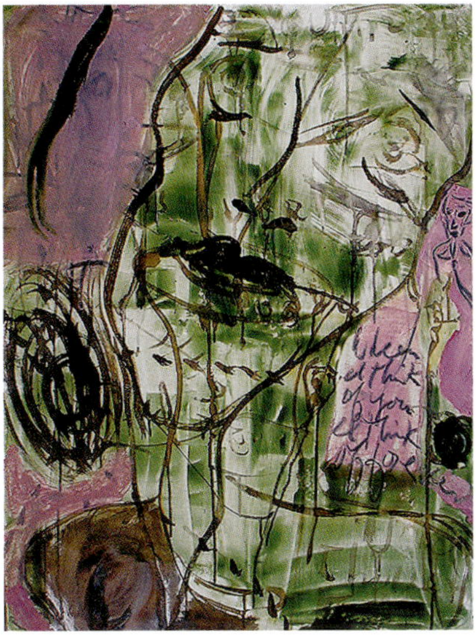

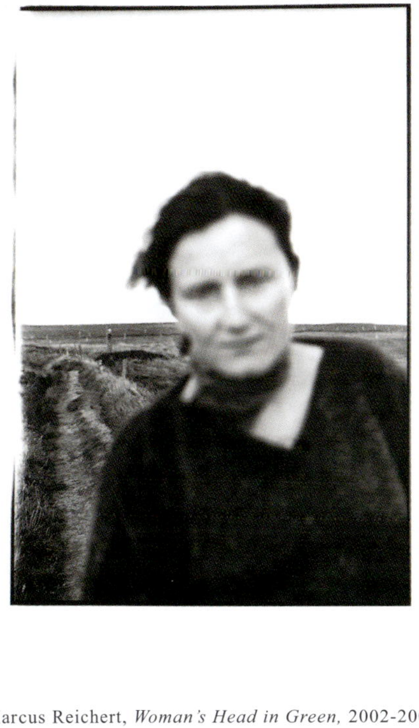

Marcus Reichert, *Woman's Head in Green,* 2002-2004
Edward Rozzo, from *Urgent Stories,* 1990-1996

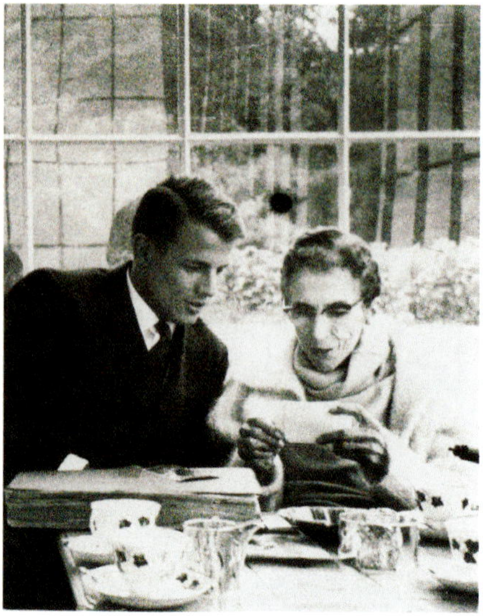

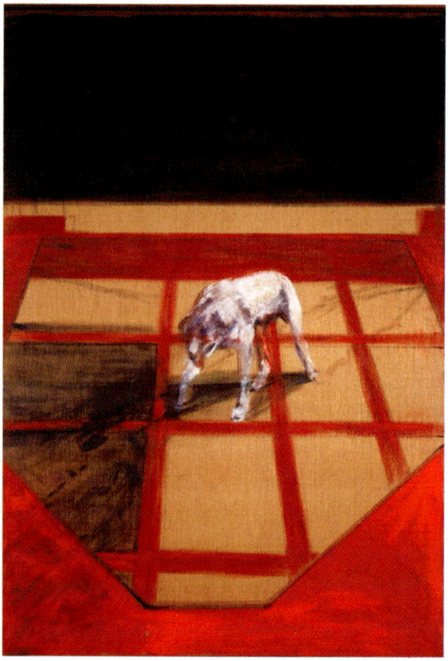

Author unknown, *Peter Beard and Isak Dinesen, Denmark,* 1961
Francis Bacon, *Dog,* 1952

of elements tends to numb.

MR: Matisse would agree. My grandmother first took me to the cinema when I was eight or nine. This was something we did on a hot summer afternoon. She lived in Levittown, New Jersey not far from the sea. Levittown was a sprawling post-war development of economically conceived houses in the *ranch house* style. It was an exotic place for my brother and me to have our summer vacation because we came from the rolling hills of Pennsylvania and that part of New Jersey is absolutely flat, almost to a disorientating degree. We would walk the long curves of those bland streets, scrubby saplings tied to wooden stakes here and there, to the shopping center. The movie theatre was very impressive, and it was air-conditioned. My grandmother always took a sweater with her. We ate popcorn and watched grown-up movies. My mother was never going to know the sort of movies we saw.

Occasionally in Pennsylvania, I went to see cowboy movies in a nearby town which had an elevated train to Philadelphia. It was the kind of place that has lots of seedy bars. The cowboy movies didn't look anything like the adult movies my grand-mother took us to. The adult movies shimmered and glowed. Black dresses rustled provocatively against grey flannel trou-sers. The images were deceptively subdued. They were sexy, so sexy that I would lie in my bed at night thinking about Suzy Parker, about what she had looked like in her underwear, as opposed to how she had looked in her evening dress. I now firmly believe that those movies corrupted my sense of colour. In my imagination, the women I had seen on the screen were a succulent rosy pink, although perhaps paler than might be considered wholesome. So when I photograph a woman in a state of undress, my determination is to make her as pale and silky as my imagination once allowed in my early adolescence. This, I think, is a good example of the psychology of colour. It is also a good example of how black and white photography can achieve something altogether different but just as powerful as colour.

ER: I think it's very intimate to understand one's relation to colour, like that succulent rosy pink of Suzy Parker's skin. I'm in love with almost all colours. I suspect this comes from my mother's desire to use colour all the time. She just loved changing the curtains, sofa covers, drapes, even her clothing. When she bought a pair of shoes, she would buy a pair in every colour they came in! My father was always furious about the money she spent, but she just loved all the colours she saw and couldn't do without them! That's me too. Most people don't enjoy such a cacophony of colour, especially in Italy. In Italy, everyone wants to be in good taste. So we have things in black and grey and white, and sometimes beige. It adds up to a very refined and beautiful use of colour, but it's also very boring in the long run. Bella figura!

Colour has always been bound up with technology and its progressive changes. After all, black and white was really the only available film up until almost the Fifties. We associate tons of things with black and white images, not because they're black and white, but because they were the only images at the time. Due to this mental warping, if it weren't for painting we'd have a hard time thinking of the mid 1800's in colour, because all we've ever seen of that period are photographs in black and white. Obviously, there's the transformation that a black and white image gives to reality. The change is obvious, so we concentrate on photographic details and are not distracted by the random colours which inhabit reality. But are those colours really as random as they seem, or are they a testimony to the technology which produces them?

MR: Knowing you, I don't imagine this to be a rhetorical question. I believe each of us has a collaboration with our colour *technology* that verges on the clandestine. I would like to think that no one knows, or could possibly understand, the rapport we have with our film stock, camera, etc. It is an eccentric relationship, which is what makes the results interesting. I can almost smell photographs that don't have this peculiar aspect to them. They often are big-time art market images. They don't tell me anything about anything except how clever, or magnificent, or sleight-of-hand they might be. Andreas Gursky is about this *shock and awe*, but after the initial *awesomeness* of the image, I don't find very much enriching about the Gursky Experience. Frankly, naming names isn't very nice, and this isn't the inquisition, this is just me reacting to what I see—having a very limited experience of the technology involved. But this does perhaps hearken back to your observations concerning narcissism: I am numbed by the complete lack of reflective intuition—emotion, if you will—in the quintessential *big-time* image. Usually, the colour in such photographs is extraordinary. It is complex and all-encompassing, but is often only that. For me, there is very little or no psychological texture in the colour of these panoramic highly-detailed images of sand dunes, blocks of apartments, shopping malls, piles of dead bodies. And often, I find something offensive about these images.

ER: For me, Gursky's images *are* interesting and arresting and not only for their technological competence. But the important question is the art market and why Gursky can make that kind of money selling images like this. That's a story which has to do with the market place, therefore with supply and demand. The interesting question to ask is *why* is society today willing to pay astronomical figures for these technically amazing images. Where is the value? That is a very interesting question because it touches the roots of culture and how we attribute value to things. So why do we value Gursky's photos so much? I think that first, OK, there's the hype. The right people are saying "these images are worth it," but the reasons are deeper. We're all little numbers in a very, very big world and Gursky's photos confirm this: that assures us. Second, their size is overwhelming, and that excites us because it gives us comfort. We say, "Yes, it's true what he's saying, there *is* a lot of repetition and *the masses* are everywhere we live!" I believe he corroborates much of our existence, and that's why people are willing to pay high prices for his images. They are easy to understand, there's no abstract reasoning, and he confirms what we believe about ourselves. I agree that he is not thought-provoking, but no one says that he has to be, so I'll accept him on that. I personally have a tougher time with the Becher photos because I really can't see what's so interesting about them. Of course, they are the teachers of Gursky, so they obviously know a lot about the art market.

But getting back to your observations about colour, I would say that each of our relationships with colour is more *intimate* than *clandestine*. I don't see anything clandestine about it, but our technical choices—our films, our cameras, our printers, our monitors, our Photoshop decisions—are all very intimate affairs. That's why you can see some sort of *style* in our work. It is imbued with dozens of choices which have more to do with our personalities than with the technologies we employ. That brings us to the *reflexivity* of identity and how we can identify who we are. Colour choices and the technologies involved are part of that reflexivity.

MR: I think your explanation for Gursky's commercial success is compelling and undoubtedly accurate. After its initial impact, I just don't find Gursky's work very interesting, and I've seen quite a few of his enormous and absolutely immaculate prints at auction houses. For me, the declension from the Bechers to Gursky is a kind of permutating deadness. Where the Bechers are stultifyingly sedate, Gursky is paradoxically bombastic. So, I really don't disagree with what you say, it's just that I don't find any of it reassuring. It relates directly to the trend in advertising at the moment (2007) to fill up the TV screen with as many similar or identical things as possible, be they people, dancing elephants, or pink soap bubbles. Although there's too much of everything, we're supposed to like it anyway. My problem is that I don't. My interpretation of your use of the word *reassuring* has more to do with acceptance, if not acquiescence.

Reflexivity of identity is terminology which is unknown to me. It does make perfect sense as you refer to it. It is about our intuition, and it is about our desire to be identified with a particular aesthetic, even though we might actually be creating that aesthetic ourselves, or tangentially contributing to the evolution of an existing aesthetic which has emerged from our well of experience. There is no denying that whatever technology we employ is a central part of realising the aesthetic, or system of aesthetics, that is our individual identity as artists. Being an artist is thought by many to be very special, and so now we have millions of artists. It's, as you might say, the way of the world. But, in a roundabout way, this brings me to the subject of the interpretation of colour, i.e. how we relate to colour. Why are some colours considered sophisticated and some not? Why are certain combinations of colours considered pleasing and some not? Why choose one colour to solve a particular problem rather than another? Why, as we were discussing before, eliminate certain colours from your composition? Why, before realising a work of art, imagine something to be one colour when in reality it simply isn't? All of these questions, I think, have to do with the psychology of colour.

ER: Sophistication in colour touches, I think, that fluid mobility of consensus which we call *taste*. Sophisticated colours change from generation to generation, and from country to country. As I've said before, I love colour. That means I love practically all colours. It's really always a matter of *context*. It's the context that makes colour acceptable or not. Garish colours are fantastic if they're not competing with other garish colours. Soft colours are magnificent if they're within subdued areas of colour. Saturated colours are rewarding if they play off each other or if they stand out on a black or neutral background. So all of them are, in their own way, exciting. The choices come really in *contexualizing* them. They stand with what other colours? Where? In what light? In what room? I believe it's the context which says it all, it's the company they keep which decides if they're in a good crowd or not. Simple relativity.

MR: Have you ever been with someone, perhaps someone you're very fond of, and they're dressed in a colour that, as far you're concerned, really doesn't suit them? It might even be so bad that the colour they're wearing in conjunction with their own coloration—for instance red hair, hazel eyes, fair freckled skin—makes you feel slightly nauseous. I would venture to say that we've all been subjected to environments that made us feel somewhat ill. Although one can't avoid another person's preference in colour as far as clothing is concerned (although one can try to talk them out of it), one can avoid places that are particularly sick-making in their palette. It may sound fanatical, and in reality it may *be* fanatical, but I try to control the colour in which I live utterly and completely, and I refuse to live with white—except for the exacting embellishment of bed linens. When I make a painting or take a photograph, this obsession remains. I'm not about to give up on someone I love simply because I can't tolerate their colour sense, but I am going to leave a room if I can't submerge its miserable colour in bonhomie or alcohol.

ER: That's the price you pay for being so sensitive to colour. It's like the guy in Oliver Sacks' book *The Man Who Mistook His Wife For A Hat*, a patient of his who after an accident acquired a dog's sense of smell. The guy smelt *everything* within a kilometre's radius. He said it was *excruciating*. He said the worst thing in the world was walking into a room full of people and all at once smelling *all* their faces. He said it stank. Well, that seems to be your reaction to colour. It's a bit like mine. One of the reasons I left America was because it was so *ugly* colourwise. Colours were used so garishly, without any idea of their worth. But I find particularly interesting your *continual* use of colours, everywhere and anywhere. It's fascinating that you use whites only for your bed linen. That's a very beautiful thing to do, and very un-iPodish. Everyone wants everything white, it's so clean, pure, spiritual! But you've got this deep sense of the emotional feelings that colours give off, so white once again regains its purity.

8.

MR: I recently wrote something for Blunt Edge 7, the yearly journal of the Peter Fuller Memorial Foundation, which read in part:

"I very seldom go to galleries or museums anymore. I don't like crowds, and I'm not particularly interested in science projects. The Guggenheim Museum in New York brings about a stuttering vertigo in me. Scale, we are assured, transcends the failings of delicacy. But I've never been to the Grand Canyon, and don't intend to go. Special EFX give me indigestion. Of course war makes the most dynamic TV, but try being there. Blood rituals no longer signify, they entertain. Hermann Nitsch[13] looks merely archaic when compared with the intricacy of slaughter on a Baghdad street. Ghouls feed on morbidity, fun-loving day-trippers feed on just about any intimidating spectacle. The trick is to make it big, perplexing, and very grand in its technological achievement. Shock and/or awe inhabits the art space."

ER: There was an interesting meeting held, I think, last year in the United States on the question of whether there should be limits to what imagery can ethically be shown in print. The question, as you say, involves not just the news industry, but society in general and the art world in particular. Before getting into details, I believe two basic elements are compounded here. One, and the most obvious, is the numbing of our feelings by the overload our nervous systems deal with all day, every day. The second element is our need for life and death emotions in everyday life. Or, should I say, *is* there a need for life and death emotions in every day life? Evidently, if you do feel overwhelmed by images of exaggerated emotional states to the point of numbness, there is. I can be disgusted by

[13] Hermann Nitsch (1938–), Austrian experimentalist artist associated with the Vienna Actionists

shocking works of art or news. In fact I avoid looking at them, but their effectiveness is corroborated by audience polls. So the question is, what can we do?

MR: Not much. If you watch the news, it's unavoidable. Television images of carnage and mayhem infest my subconscious. These images mingle with my own peculiar psychology and emerge in my dreaming. So when we talk about the "surge of anxiety which fills the present", which is an unavoidable reality in a world dominated by the media, we are actually talking about *feeding* on the haphazard destruction meted out by humanity—and it's the media's job to make it palatable. Similarly, it's the curator's job to make sense of nonsensical art. In the same article for Blunt Edge, I also wrote:

"*Grotesque* often has its own peculiar dignity, as in Picasso, but then of course Picasso made paintings, not meticulous replicas of aeroplane crashes and dismembered children. Then there is *conscience*, an elusive artistic pursuit at best. But conscience occupies a hallowed space of its own, and when conscience informs social commentary destined for the galleries, out come the trowels and up go the gargantuan digital screens. Regardless of the moral fibre required to grapple with the saddest subjects, the triumph of artifice is assured."

You as a photographer are obliged to perfect your ideas and imagery via technology, and technology of a very sophisticated nature. Do you feel that there is an essential corruption of poetic vision in this process? In other words, do you feel that the vulnerability that informs our moral objectivity is diluted or lost in the process of realising a more or less perfectly executed project?

ER: I don't personally feel that the technological side of photography is in any way corrupting, just as I don't feel that *any* technology is corrupting. If anything, it's enriching because it extends my capabilities. Words, in a certain sense, are technology, so where's the corruption? As to the *conscience* that you speak about. When you speak derisively of aeroplane crashes and dismembered children being shown as art, Maurizio Catalan comes to mind. What I'm thinking of is a very contested installation he did here in Milano in the middle of a very big plaza. He hung three dummies of children from the central tree as if they had been lynched. They were happy children simply lynched in one of the central piazzas of Milano. All hell broke loose and he was forced to take them down in less than a day. One guy even broke a couple of bones climbing the tree in order to cut the children dummies down. This took place during the invasion of Iraq.

Setting aside any questions concerning the personality of Maurizio Catalan, I was shocked to see the installation—I saw it being hung as I passed by in a tram—but I can't but applaud the artistic intention. Here's an artist who manages to bring fundamental questions concerning ethics into the foreground of social thought by creating a provocative but apparently innocent installation. Nice looking kids hung from a tree. It *was* shocking, but shouldn't it have been? Why aren't we as shocked by the hundreds of Iraqi children killed so mercilessly in a war? How can you address this situation on a public scale? Catalan did. He found a way to create a very effective reminder of what is really happening in the world, and he didn't use any blood, gore, or spilling guts. He just found the right idea. I'm all for that. Was this piece *grotesque*? In a certain sense, yes. Did it *work*, as we used to say in art school? Yes, I think it really did.

MR: This is of course an altogether different proposition than creating such an installation in a pristine public art gallery—where there is no real impact, where the shock is largely gratuitous because the viewer is engaged primarily in contemplating the aesthetic attributes of the work. Bringing this representation of man's shameful behaviour, obviously as manifest in this time-frame by the American government, to the unsuspecting people of Milano is a brilliant way to get them to focus on the suffering of people in another city in another part of the world. It makes someone else's suffering an intimate experience.

When you refer without comment to the personality of Maurizio Catalan, something else I've been thinking about quite a lot comes to mind: it would be absurd to deny that the compulsion to expose one's art is about the ego. Of course it's a cliché, but everyone is now allowed to be *an artist* and it doesn't look like this perception is going to change any time soon. The preening results are overwhelming in their number and diversity. The entertainment factor is truly limitless. But how does the artist use his art to justify his existence, an existence which might otherwise appear to be utterly and completely without meaning, like the supposedly uneventful life of everyone else?

ER: I've been battling this question my whole life. The reason I *didn't* become an artist was because I couldn't justify to myself, my Calvinistic self, that this level of egocentric attention was acceptable. Now, at 60, I know that I was wrong. But the problem is that one has to be mature enough to *know* that it's okay from the start and I certainly didn't arrive at any state of maturity until I was over 40. So I didn't plan my artistic career. I didn't invest in shows, rather I threw myself into my professional work. I felt that it was there that I should leave my mark. Now that I know that in the commercial world no one looks carefully at what you do, and after one fiscal year whatever you did is just trash, I think that *maybe* I should have chosen the other route—that of the artist. On the other hand, as you say, it *does* seem to be utterly meaningless unless you do a lot of thinking and come to a justifying conclusion. This, by the way, is fairly improbable, given the uncertainties of the art world and the fragility of the human psyche. So we're back to zero.

MR: From where I'm sitting it would appear that the art world has managed to contrive its own elitist state, with an irrefutable structure of hierarchies, confirming the artist in his significance. Or has the art world grown organically and miraculously from the seeds sown by such conceptual wizards as André Breton and Marcel Duchamp, so that the artist himself is only interesting in his usefulness to the system, like a drone bee?

ER: I would add Marinetti,[14] even if he was a Fascist fanatic with all the arrogance and unjustifiable ignorance that that brings with it. But the real push for today's artists came after the Second World War with the "baby boomers" and the rise of the institutional Art School. Art Schools have been manufacturing artists for over fifty years. All of these *artists* vie for our attention. They all want a piece of the pie. Most give up, some throw in the towel, eliminating themselves in the process, some are around teaching, and some are showing their work.

MR: You mention how artists vie for attention, and that's really what the contemporary art world is about—that, and making money. I'm referring to what they call today *careerists*. These are the artists who have a strategy. They see their art developing in logical stages, and there must always be an evolving aspect to what they do. There must be development, there must also be what Clement Greenberg[15] referred to as the artist's *breakthrough*. These are the artists who took instruction in how *to be* artists. Not everyone adheres to this school of thought. And some of us find it downright dreary.

ER: That artists today are professional careerists, just like everyone else, is a fact. Whether you draw illustrations for the shopping mall or hang your stuff on a wall, you're in a profession because you're working to sell what you do. The fact that you might have to think harder or try to be at one with your instinctive self doesn't eliminate the fact that you are somehow

[14] Filippo Tommaso Emilio Marinetti (1876–1944), Italian idealogue, editor, poet, and founder of the futurist movement

[15] Clement Greenberg (1909–1994), American art critic of the abstract movement

part of a society that uses or at least wants your work in some way. I can understand that this might be a dreary idea, but it's what the Western world is about: economy.

MR: Perhaps that's the problem with the Western world.

ER: From what I know of you, I think your desire and actual life plan is more like that of a philosopher than an artist in a contemporary way. You're looking to visualise things which do not necessarily have a name or a verbal logic. You're looking to work through intuition in order to have some kind of revelation. That's very exciting and very useful, but unless you convince others as to its usefulness (mental and spiritual) then your work simply sits in your studio.

MR: Like most painters who live a relatively obscure life, I prefer to let someone else do the convincing. It's these people—who do the convincing—who are invaluable, because they know we have to survive and they are willing to help. If their motivation is economical, to use your line of thinking, one hopes the work isn't somehow misrepresented. By the way, I can't say I've ever had a "life plan." I've been obliged by circumstance to take things as they come and make whatever adjustments might be necessary simply to survive. Thankfully, my life is somewhat easier now.

ER: But there's nothing wrong with having a strategy or a life plan. People who live their lives to gain success or money have to make tons of choices like you and I, it's just that often they have a different set of values. So what? It might be dreary to you because you'd like to think that people are intelligent enough to understand what you and others are doing without having to put it through the economic grinder, but it's just a way of understanding value. Otherwise how could you possibly judge what you do? Against whose set of values?

MR: I don't judge what I do by someone else's system of values, I judge what I do by studying the work and reasoning with myself. How could anyone possibly achieve anything interesting or original by adhering to someone else's idea of what is worthwhile, even acceptable? The "economic grinder" can be very destructive. Economic success, which I'm obviously not at all opposed to, encourages imitation of both one's own work and the work of other economically successful artists. Certainly, I take inspiration from other painters and poets but the majority of them are dead and therefore, to my way of thinking, sacrosanct and beyond imitation. They may be archetypes but they are benign. As we re-enforce our own identity, we drift farther and farther away from what is known, and what is known to be acceptable in the marketplace. We risk catastrophe but occasionally the rewards can be exceptional. Isolation is quite often not a bad thing.

ER: We're still all a bit victims of the romantic idea of the artist being discovered and being in some way a seer. Actually, one simply chooses one's profession, and being an artist is a very rewarding one if you're not too much into commercial success. If you are into commercial success, well then you've got to be a strategist about yourself and your work.

MR: But it's tedious. Most art, if one were to stare reality in the face, is basically about showing off, about proving how clever one is. There must be some relevance to what you call *visual fallout* but it's not the sort of thing I think about. I think about not knowing why I'm doing something, and try to understand both why I'm doing that something *and* why I don't know why. This is the conundrum for the artist who works through his intuition. As odd as it may seem, I heard Richard Serra[16] saying the same thing on TV the other evening. The thing about Serra is that he takes his little impulses and writes them very large in ponderous amounts of metal.

ER: Visual fallout goes forwards and backwards from thought or instinct into art then illustration then, sometimes, into

[16] Richard Serra (1939–), American minimalist sculptor and video artist

advertising where it can go back into art. Look at some of the fantastic work of Barbara Kruger.

MR: I've seen Kruger's work. It's very *knowing*.

ER: Kruger's work *is* knowing in as much as she has a concrete idea of what's happening in society. You might not agree with her, but she is into communications. Someone's got to do it.

MR: I can't see that there's anything to agree or disagree *with*. Perhaps it's just that I don't find her work very revealing of anything but the banal. When I confront works like *You Will Never Wake Up From This Dream* (title within frame and postcard roses on a baby blue ground) or *Sex/Lure* (title within frame and square jaw and full masculine lips isolated in austere browns and greys) and think on the obviousness of the message in conjunction with the obviousness of the imagery, I can only conclude that these works have been contrived for a clientele that wants to be reminded of what it already knows. Basically, Kruger has nothing to say about or for herself, unless of course you find a plethora of clichés profound. As you and I don't agree on the importance of Barbara Kruger's work, what sort of innovation have you found particularly stimulating?

ER: I think of the importance of Giotto introducing his *own* friends into his painting to substitute the traditional imaginary non-specific faces while telling the story of Jesus. That *visualisation* changed the immediacy of religion within the minds and hearts of the hundreds and then thousands of people who saw his work. Or Correggio's *Assumption of the Virgin*[17] in the Parma Cathedral here in Italy. This was practically the *first* painting where you didn't have to know the story portrayed or the symbolism included to understand it, you simply had to

[17] Antonio Allegri da Correggio (1489–1534), Italian Renaissance painter

look at it and you were emotionally taken in. These are things that change the individual's perception of his role in society, that change society in general.

MR: Correggio is one thing but Caravaggio[18] is another. Caravaggio loved beautiful boys, when it was officially forbidden, and he loved the danger of risking the trust of others. He had criminal tendencies which I can altogether appreciate.

ER: Caravaggio was a character, but he sure knew how to paint shadows! Of course, the artist's level of personal indulgence was born out of the human need to speak to God on a one to one basis. Painting biblical stories was also a way of relating to God. Caravaggio was very interested in how God dealt with human nature since it might be a way of dealing with himself. That is, the artist fell in with the rest of society trying to *relate* to the world outside by working through the socially accepted dogma of the times.

MR: Perhaps when Caravaggio was locked in that sewer-pit in Malta after one of his violent rages, he spoke to God. But, I would imagine, he gave up the dialogue shortly after being extracted from his hole. I once spoke to God in the midst of a nervous breakdown. He said, Go across town to Lenox Hospital, which is open in the middle of the night for business, and get yourself some drugs. I wish I knew more about other lost souls who have spoken with God.

ER: That depends on your meaning of *God*. The little distinctions—who is God, where is God, etc.—have done wonders for people interested in selling arms. But, if you trace the roots of our relationship to God, they've also done wonders for our individuality.

---

[18] Michelangelo Merisl de Caravaggio (1571–1610), Italian painter of the Baroque school

MR: My disenchantment with religion occurred with a prolonged identification with Christ at the age of eleven or twelve. I had the overwhelming feeling that I too would be sacrificed, but I would be sacrificed for the simple fact of being alive. My own life would end for no particular reason, and so everything I experienced would be almost unbearably exquisite but meaningless, and especially meaningless because I simply couldn't believe there was a God who would grant me eternal life. There would be no reprieve, death would be my final blessing. My dialogue with God became increasingly abstract, until now I am consumed by the abstraction of life. I might be tempted to say that I speak to God in all things if I didn't find the idea of such a dialogue totally without empathy or reason, especially when I consider the magnitude of suffering in the world—I find this abstract dialogue within myself almost too precious and self-indulgent to bear. My belief is that Jesus Christ also gave up the idea of God.

ER: We're into liquid modernity and here we are, all sloshing around in cosmic toothpaste wondering who's holding the cosmic toothbrush. Well, I'm pretty much with Thomas Aquinas on this one. The life within us *is* God and our thinking and expressing ourselves is part of the miracle. So we've gone from Aquinas's illumination—*everyone* is the presence of God—to *everyone* is an artist.

MR: And how has this self-divinity effected your vision as an artist, perhaps even more importantly as a person?

ER: I have much more respect for every little image I make now. It's all part of my living thought.

MR: I like this expression, living thought, but can only suppose what it means for you. For me, "living thought" would be what modernists between the wars called one's stream of consciousness.[19] Virginia Woolf disliked this term, possibly because she hadn't coined it herself, but occasionally wrote at great length in a form that can only be described as that.

ER: Living thought isn't really stream of consciousness, it's a choice of narrative. I can be very aware of what I'm doing and thinking and separate what I express from what I feel. Thinking is not as easy as it seems, nor is transmitting ideas to others. I only learned to think late in my life. For the first forty years I just flipped through the pages. This all came to an end when I almost died of pneumonia at the age of 42. I began to understand what thinking is about. I would sit very still during my recovery and think. I realised that thinking is a wonderful occupation and that it holds the key to understanding. This realisation astonished me. My intimate feelings and emotions are interesting to someone else only if I've understood their relation to bigger problems than *myself*. That's why I feel the need to share things I feel might be useful to someone else. In that sense, I've always found photography particularly *revealing*. I think a photographic image reveals new relationships between things we see and things we ignore. It can also show us things we see all the time in a very different way, thus enabling us to delve into a deeper significance within everyday life. Now I don't know if some would call that relating to God or simply relating to a larger aspect of society. I don't particularly care what might be said, but I believe that our exchange of feelings and thoughts is a very deep and important part of living. So my living thoughts are things I visually show to others while I'm thinking about life. It's like showing someone an interesting pebble on a beach.

MR: What you describe is very closely aligned to my determination to make photographs that the viewer can walk into, photographs that are empty spaces waiting to be inhabited by

[19] This expression attributed to May Sinclair, pseudonym of Mary Amelia St. Clair (1862–1946), British writer

the spirit of the person who happens upon that place. What I feel when I am in that place and decide to take the photograph is what I want to convey. And, invariably, like your pebble on the beach, it's the sensation and the character of the thing that I want to reveal. *Living thought* is what it is, and if there is anything at all sublime about these revelations they will continue to live in our thoughts—no matter how our circumstances might conspire to submerge them.

9.

MR: I am curious to know why you are so respectful of Philip-Lorca diCorcia's work. Is he not simply a photographer who had to find a way to take a picture that would be sensational? This is what he is doing today, case in point being the theatrically lit pole-dancers hanging on their ropes. Most puzzling for me is his work involving male prostitutes. But these pictures are his most beautiful because they have a certain childlike fragility which hinges on fantasy. However, I too often find the humanity in these images obscured by artifice. I feel the same about Gregory Crewdson. Taking cinema into the realm of still photography may be exciting but, for me, nothing is as good as the reality itself, especially as glimpsed by a poetic mind (like William Eggleston's, or Brassaï's, or Weegee's or, to an especially disconcerting degree, Nan Goldin's). For me the problem is sensationalist mentality. Yes, diCorcia's images are arresting, but I find no solace or real exhilaration in them.

ER: Let's start with the male prostitutes series. I'm not particularly crazy about these images, although they are very well lit and staged, but this puts on the line the selling of human pleasure, which is always a theme of social interest both for the needs of sex as well as the self-deprecation necessary to accomplish the job. That, in itself, is why I believe these images are interesting. The series also came along when "staging" was emerging as a new concept and theoretical prominence was given to the unreality of reality and to the apparently false imagery of profound feelings that photography can yield. Add to that the fact that no one would have imagined that the phenomena of male prostitution dealt with people our age (at the time) who looked relatively cool most of the time. The simple descriptive aspect of the work played well on the darker side of trendy art imbued with homosexual fantasy and male power.

MR: I think what you say is both accurate and sympathetic, but I am most impressed with your reference to the fantasy aspect of these images, and I can't help but think of them as *romantic*. For me, everything about them contrives to create a kind of romantic atmosphere, even though it might superficially seem sordid or bleak. They are indeed complex. DiCorcia's ethereal lighting certainly contributes to the unreality of what otherwise would be a stark proposition.

ER: But the work of real interest is the street photographs and the later street portraits. These images look very staged and the people in them look very much like actors on a stage. Simple. Shakespeare. Easy to understand. Easy to look at, but also very near the pathos of the human bewilderment in post-modern society. People who are lost, rushing along the street, going somewhere they think is very important but is really just self-related. Here we have images which give a 'visualisation' of what this is all about. Here we have a photographer who looks at the very banal situation of living in the year 2000 on a street—throughout major capitals in the world—and shows us an incredible staged setting where we all play out our lives. His technique is such that he creates a new aesthetic language in street photography. Staged, artificially lit, non-events with insignificant people becoming the major actors in a play they don't even know exists. That's why his work, I think, is important. He's got away from the self-centred universe of narcissism and self-narration and he's given us a vision of ourselves in a metaphysically disturbing way. Something like the anguish in a Francis Bacon painting. Here we have 21st century people simply lost and striving on a street, numbed to the role they play and no longer aware of what is happening. In fact, in one of his earlier street images, there is a marquee of a theatre playing *The Waste Land*.

MR: Perhaps what is most lacking today is what I can only call a self-effacing honesty, which undoubtedly most successful artists would secretly consider counter-productive, if not downright self-destructive. You mention Francis Bacon, and when you look at the earlier paintings, there is a wilful denial of any acceptable or lauded form. He is saying that our culture derives from the realisations of the individual, no matter how awkward or painful those realisations might be. Bacon's images are obviously staged, and, yes, I do see this in diCorcia's images of people in the street, although he has accomplished this via subterfuge (i.e. via his lighting technique and "caught" framing). For me, these images *are* arresting, but rather than find them revealing of very much, I find them numbing. Yes, the fact of what futile lives we lead is numbing. The fact of our shared needs and expendability is numbing. The compression of the universe is numbing. Numbers are numbing, and diCorcia has captured the anonymity of our existence, something we dare not admit to ourselves. For me, Walker Evans' subway riders are far more moving in this regard. DiCorcia seems to be asking: is life an empty proposition in which we are made to perform? Certainly, in the harsh light of what we all know as so-called artists, diCorcia enlivens *himself* in the exposition of our absurdity.

ER: You mentioned the "sensationalist mentality" consistent with a society which cries out for shocking ideas and stunning presentation, and you mentioned Gregory Crewdson. I'm not down on Crewdson either, but I find his work much less interesting than diCorcia's simply because diCorcia limits himself to simpler themes and then explores them better. There's still a bit of the unexpected in diCorcia whereas with Crewdson it's like watching a movie without all the sounds and movement. So I find him less interesting.

MR: I can't recall anyone saying this but many photographers, it seems, are frustrated film directors. Most film directors are frustrated photographers, especially because they must make their images through the director of photography—this relationship had therefore better be a profoundly sympathetic one. Pornography in photography obviously has a lot to do with this. Going to the cinema must drive some photographers round the bend. Suffice it to say, all imagery is now cinemagraphic. And when it isn't—I mean purposefully so—it strikes one as unduly arid, like creating a composition simply for the sake of creating a composition. The film still as abstracted through still photography (fine art photography) is, I agree, a worthwhile pursuit. This occurs, I hope subtly, in my own photographs. Many of my images are simply missing the actors.

ER: As to the solace you ask for, should we look at this stuff to find solace? I'm not sure. Maybe I look more towards the spirit or philosophy to find solace and more towards the contemporary art scene to see thoughts worked through and splattered before my eyes, helping me to rethink things I thought I understood or things I haven't found a visualisation for yet. But if you accept a Nan Goldin, why not accept a diCorcia? I find solace, if you will, in the communal fact that we are *all* like people in DiCorcia's photographs. And that makes me feel more part of something than the usual exclusion my misanthropy often creates in my mind.

MR: When I used the word *solace* I was referring to a philosophical state of mind rather than a psychological one, although they are perhaps in reality inseparable! What I meant to say is that I do not find the sort of very particular expression I am looking for in very many of these photographs. There is great resolve in their conception and execution, but is any particular state of mind made known, even obliquely, that we can inhabit within ourselves? We inhabit a place and a time—an atmosphere—when we look at these pictures, but do we take away the conjurings of an individual who is really coming to terms with anything? It's not that I don't accept what diCorcia does, it's just that it feels so very obvious and I can't quite get round that. If anything, his images encourage and enhance my misanthropy. When I watch advertising on TV and see how nearly everything being sold is being promoted with masses and masses of things—crowds swarming in the streets below us, animated arrows flying everywhere, hundreds of shiny bubbles and dancing flowers, transfixed teenagers marching—I am revolted and numbed by the pride humanity takes in its mere existence.

ER: It's true that diCorcia's work certainly doesn't help us in any way, but his visualisations, I think, are not only arresting but significant. As to photographers wanting to be filmmakers, maybe, maybe not. You see how the fixed image acquires a mystique and depth that no film image gains unless stopped and put on a wall. On the other hand, how can anything compete with film as an all encompassing medium? But back to diCorcia's prostitute series. Why idolise, as diCorcia's photos do, a prostitute? Why idolise people who sell themselves to make a living? It's outside of any logic, religious vision, or good common sense. And yet, these people, these young prostitutes *are* idolised and glorified by diCorcia's work. They're like Hollywood stars due to their lighting, staging and presentation. They are almost unsung heroes. I think this response to these images comes from the moral and sexual confusion which has highlighted certain aspects of self-punishment as glamour. It's like the adolescent desire to risk death in order to *feel* something because otherwise life is boring and uneventful. These images play into that kind of undeclared need to give meaning to life. So what's sex worth? $22 or $50 for twenty minutes? Is an orgasm what life is about?

MR: Perhaps it is, but it takes various unacknowledged forms. Committing murder is certainly a kind of orgasm. Adolescents join the army to—on some ridiculous level—fuck around with their own mortality. Most armies now are aggregations of hired killers, only the would-be killers are poor misguided kids, no matter how smart they look in their cool uniforms and Ray-Bans. They're encouraged to get off on violence, to kick in doors and people's faces. We are *embedded* with them. We are meant to share their orgasm.

ER: The more desperate the audience, the more an orgasm is what life's about. It's like passion, if you're not desperate emotionally it just doesn't happen. If you are . . . watch out. Some people also believe that passionate love is the pinnacle of human existence, like the myth of the simultaneous orgasm. It's certainly the pinnacle of emotional symbiosis with the universe, but it's a far cry from the pinnacle of human existence. So to get back on the ground, I agree with you that these images are a bit on the *cheap thrill* side.

MR: It occurs to me that diCorcia's dangling pole-dancers are his answer to the photographs of Sapporo bondage I so treasured in my teens. They were the most exotic thing I'd ever seen, but I was most drawn to the women's faces. I can't now gaze upon an image of a geisha without simultaneously imaging her in a state of abject subservience, which is a grotesque state of mind and, most importantly, an artificial one, because I find Japanese women especially beautiful without any sense of titillation whatsoever. DiCorcia might, if he were here in this room, explain that these very melodramatic images are not meant to titillate but confuse, in fact meant to thwart any compulsion to orgasm. Who knows?

10.

MR: In your list of possible subjects for this dialogue, you suggested we discuss what painting is worth, and to whom and why. You also suggested we talk about the iconography of Christianity. To my way of thinking these two subjects in their diversity are obliquely but compellingly interlocking. I will try to explain.

Although I cherish the sensual attributes of painting, I am most interested in painting that is a spiritual pursuit, no matter how subliminally. I believe that as such painting serves to refresh the viewer, it has the capability of bringing submerged realms of sensation back into focus. How this is achieved is really anyone's guess, so there is an atavistic aspect to painting that runs counter to other more technologically evolved forms of expression, like photography, like cinema. It is an altogether elusive medium, while being confoundingly physical at the same time. As regards its transcendent qualities, painting is like making a new language written with the blood of past generations.

Each time a painting is made, the possibilities are limitless, whereas while the possibilities inherent in other media may also be limitless, they are nevertheless subject to the strictures of reality in its plasticity. In essence, painting is a manifestation of one's belief in the paradox of true expression. Obviously, a painting can be a literal description of something, but this is not nearly so interesting as an evocation. Evocation suits the medium in its viscosity and its fluidity. It would seem proven by history that painting is invaluable to mankind, at least to mankind as we have known it. Possessing paintings of a sublimely inspirational nature, no matter how confounding, has become central to the mythos of both public and private institutions, i.e. museums and corporations. One is tempted to suppose that the world has found an alternative to traditional religious iconography.

ER: Well, religious and secular iconography are one and the same thing. One signifier is merely substituted for another, but the emotional meaning remains very similar. We need symbols to evoke, as you say, feelings which otherwise have difficulty surfacing in daily life. I think you speak very beautifully about painting and that kind of understanding would help anyone *see* better. Sure, it's easier to take a photograph than paint, but doing something significant is just as elusive in either medium. The process as a spiritual search is, I believe, very similar. I'm not sure that technology has much to do with this. You need techniques to paint and you need techniques to photograph or to write. Does it matter what keyboard you're using? Is choosing a piece of reality less spiritual than putting pigment onto a canvas? It might seem so, but revelation is a continuing process that involves everything you see. But why, do you think, is photography so *in* and painting so *difficult* in today's world?

MR: Firstly, I want to make it clear that I don't think choosing a piece of reality with which to make a photograph is any less spiritual than making a painting. Both disciplines are naturally an extension of seeing. The big difference for me is the visceral aspect of painting—there is no immaculate conception in painting as there is in photography. This brings me to your question, which I don't understand completely because I don't believe painting is at all difficult in today's world, at least not for many professional painters. Professional painters are certified artists. They tend not to make mistakes because they have a well thought out program. That's their job—to make paintings of irrefutably good quality. They don't fuck up because their procedures won't allow them to fuck up. It's a matter for the viewer to decide if the painting is worth looking at or not. Most people who go to museums and galleries believe that there is something interesting about *any* painting. They are there to discover what painting is about, to discover what is exciting at the moment. In this context I am reminded of a statement you made regarding trends in manufactured colour, because this statement relates very much to the mentality of the professional painter:

"(Trends in colour are) part of our late capitalist economy. You know how trends are made in the industry—people study the presence of elements in society which have emerged culturally and socially, then they analyse these elements, associating them with the colours present, and then shape and sell the results to the industries which produce trends, like fashion and design. In that way, the production and preparation of products with "trendy" colours can commence a couple of years ahead of time. Otherwise nothing would be ready at the right time. It's not that these people *decide* the trend, but they dedicate themselves to *interpreting* trends that they feel are already emerging in society. Take for instance wearing ball caps or oversized pants. Those were trends seen in specific locations and then globalised for profit. The same with colours. This year the colour might be subdued oranges, browns and blacks, in three years it might be bright blues and greens. But these changes, which seem so superfluous, are actually somewhat synchronised with changing tastes. It's all quite complicated, but very real. I find myself falling in love with certain colours which I'd never noticed before, like deep salmon or electric subdued greens."

And museum-goers increasingly find themselves falling in love with this season's exciting new mode of painting. Trends in painting are big news, and they're big business. There is an awful lot of painting now that is "idea" art. Idea art is about succeeding in the big bad art world. But painting doesn't have to be like this to succeed—to succeed as painting. My inclination at this moment is to quote myself: "On the one hand, painting is a sensual pursuit, on the other, it is an avowedly intimate revealing of one's self. What I mean is that making a painting—the kind I make—is a kind of stripping away of the thick skin we develop to survive in a world increasingly uninterested in dignified personal revelation—poetry, if you will. That stripping away, in psychological terms, can be just as violent as the world is violent. It occurs to me that this is an equation of sorts. So when you ask how exactly my painting is "psychologically referential" the answer must be, as Jackson Pollock says, that the painting is a living manifestation of not only what I might reveal but also what the viewer brings to it."[20] The sort of painting I'm interested in is vulnerable, just as the painter is vulnerable *and* fallible.

Yes, photography is *in*. This is undoubtedly one of the reasons my photographs are now being seen, which is downright pecu-iar when they weren't intended for anyone to see. I took, and take, photographs only because I feel compelled to. They have absolutely no use. If someone wants to look at them, that's not something I object to anymore. There was a time when I would have objected to anyone seeing them, because many of them are extremely personal—they are about my need to know that the world exists and that it is beautiful. Sometimes, I'm not so sure about this, sometimes I think the world is essentially a very frightening place. My photographs take me back into this mystery. A good photograph is about this mystery, it somehow makes this mystery accessible to the viewer. Peter Beard's photographs convince me that Africa exists, that elephants are among nature's most majestic creatures. His photographs also convince me of man's barbarism. Peter Beard's photographs objectify all of these realisations, and they are his embodiment.

ER: I want to go back to my questioning why painting is so *difficult* today. What I mean is simply that there is a smaller public viewing painting and getting involved with painting than there was fifty or a hundred years ago. It seems to me that painting has *stepped down* for a while as a major vehicle of communication. For the most part, it has been taken over by photography, cinema, and television. Painting is more esoteric. It's for a more elite public, like most contemporary art. The public, generally speaking, hasn't been *upgraded* to what's happening in painting. If something is *evidently* nice to look

---

[20] Conversation from the Margins, *Displaced Person: Poetry, Pornography & Politics*, Marcus Reichert, Ziggurat Books, London, 2006

at and interesting, like Jean-Michel Basquiat or Keith Haring, then everyone loves it. If, on the other hand, the artist is conducting a more subtle or delicate conversation with himself and his viewers, then he's more likely known to the art galleries but not to the public. Photography is known by practically everyone because it relates to actual vision, and everyone takes an interest in seeing what's happening.

MR: I can't say I agree with very much of what you say. If anything, painting has found a larger audience in the last fifty to one hundred years. Painting has been freed from the strictures of realism, and is therefore now able to communicate on a far more intimate psychological level; so that much of what you say about the artist conducting a more subtle dialogue with the viewer is true, however people are far more fascinated by their relationship to painting now than they were when the subject of the painting was superficially a literal depiction of an event, or a person, or, for that matter, an object. As you said yourself of Correggio's *Assumption of the Virgin* in the Cathedral in Parma: "This was practically the *first* painting where you didn't have to know the story portrayed or the symbolism included to understand it, you simply had to *look* at it and you were emotionally taken in."

Jean-Michel Basquiat's painting was evidently *not nice* to look at when it first appeared, precisely because it had an impact on people that was somewhat disturbing, perhaps at times even unpleasant. I haven't any comment on Keith Haring because I don't regard him as a painter, I regard him as a cartoonist. Painting provides a kind of stimulation that is completely different than the stimulation one gets from a photograph or from going to the cinema. Painting is a language unto itself and now an increasing number of people recognise this and, perhaps most importantly, are willing to try to understand it. It's not for nothing that a Francis Bacon painting recently sold at Sotheby's for $52,600,000, or that Pablo Picasso is known to more people than Pablo Casals.

ER: Painting is semiotically more complex. It's harder to define its meaning to a large group of people. Also photography, as well as cinema and even more so television, deal with things that happen in the world. So it's easier to relate to them on a superficial level. Philip-Lorca diCorcia's photos of male prostitutes deal with prostitution and everyone can understand that. Whereas your work deals with the metaphysical relationship between your life and other people's lives, and between colours, objects, and spaces. All of this is a bit more elusive. Let's face it, people are *not* habituated to understand what they see: they look, try to figure out what they're looking at, and if they can't, they simply look the other way. This cultural laziness is part of our fragmented fast frame culture. Zap. Zap. Zap. What happened? Oh well, we're on to the next thing.

MR: There's something else here though that you're not addressing: the intuitive organisation of any visual statement. It's this intuitive organisation that communicates subliminally with the viewer. There is a psychological aspect to the organisation and realisation of the image that either makes sense to the viewer or it doesn't—it doesn't matter if we're looking at a photograph, a painting, or the moving frame of a film. I would have to say its a matter of sensual and intellectual preference. Some people are more excited by painting than photography. I believe it's just that simple. But what's interesting is that some people find certain photographs "painterly" just as some people find some paintings "factual." This is the paradox that has brought all of this image-making into focus, and especially for the viewer who wants to know more about the world and himself through the experience of someone else's vision.

ER: Painting is a slower process, a more intuitive one at this point in history. I think it's linked to feelings in the public and ideas in the critic. As the painter, you're outside of this kind of thinking because the process itself has its own rewards. But, as I've said before, you're more a philosopher or a meditator on life, and that makes you an extremely interesting artist.

MR: I don't think being "interesting" puts me outside the realm of objective thinking. Perhaps I'm less inclined to adhere to or respect a *formulaic* approach to making images. In other words, I don't trust what someone else tells me has been proven to affect the viewer in a particular way. I don't believe the experience of a visual work of art can be controlled in this way. However, what worries me is the stereotyping and imitation of powerful images which are in themselves too mysterious for this sort of political or economic manipulation. I believe we have to remain at a certain remove to have any clear or compelling idea of what's going on.

ER: As a photographer I'm not sure where I stand. I'm a bit overwhelmed by the *trends* in the art market. A very famous photographer once told me that my photographs were too full of false colours. He said that any photographer using exaggerated techniques was simply one who wanted to be an artist but didn't know how. I don't believe that. My use of photography is totally a way for me to try and understand what's happening with my life. I deal with subjects that open profound questions for me. When I've understood a question better, I abandon the subject. That's not really the way to construct a career as an artist. But I feel very close to my work, both professionally and personally.

MR: I think this very famous photographer was only interested in making photographs one way—his way. Because he was a famous photographer he thought he knew something you didn't. This sort of person is a fool. When you speak of "subjects that open profound questions" for you, I would have to say that this is the spiritual aspect of your work that I see, and that I respect. Your work is unafraid.

ER: As to the spiritual aspect of your work and your way of working, I can completely identify with that. Making photographs *is* about trying to understand. The spiritual quest, I believe, is also about trying to understand. I'm not a documentary photographer, although my images document things. I, like you, make images to play, to think, to try and understand, to pose a question. What is this space about? What do these objects mean? Why are these people in this situation? Where did this come from?

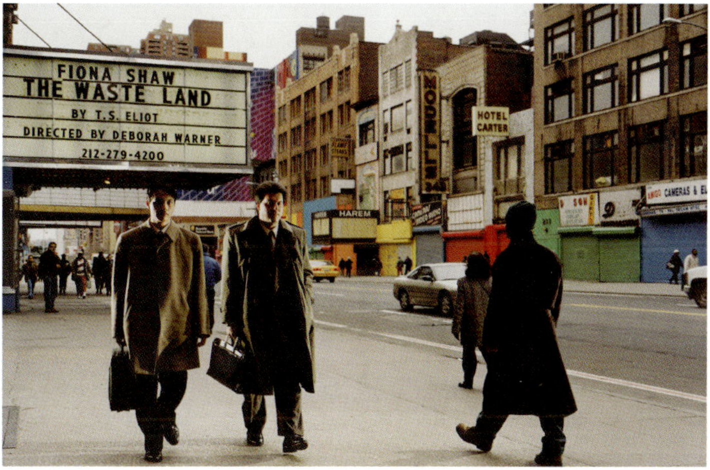

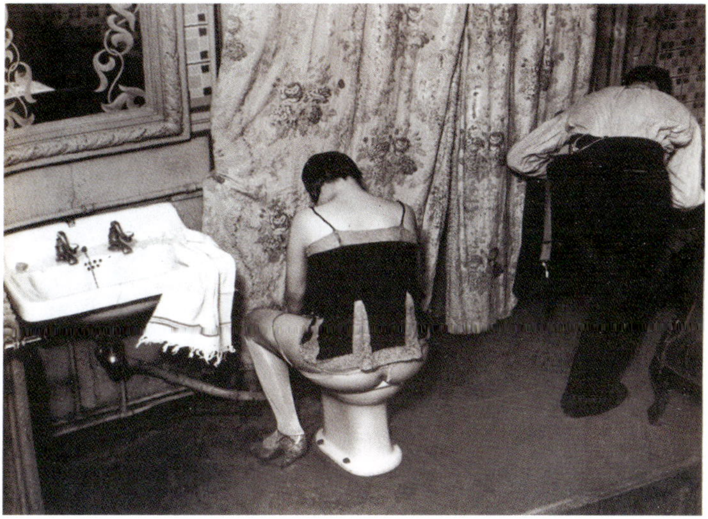

Philip-Lorca diCorcia, *New York*, 1997
Brassaï, *Washing up in a brothel, Rue Quincampoix*, c.1932

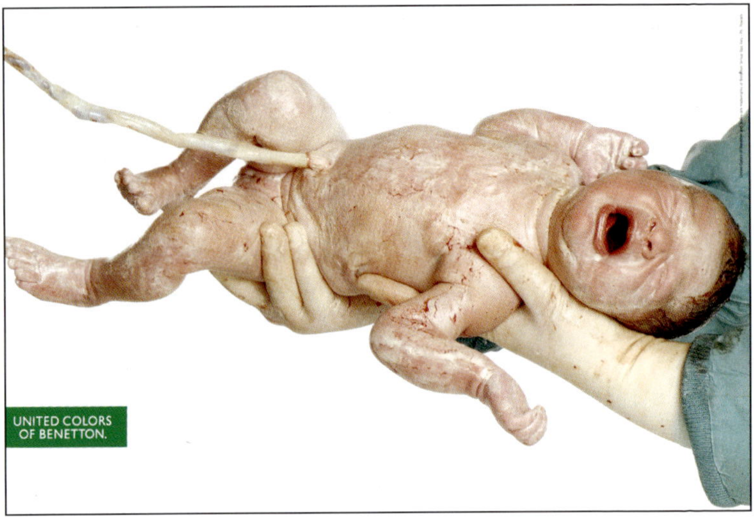

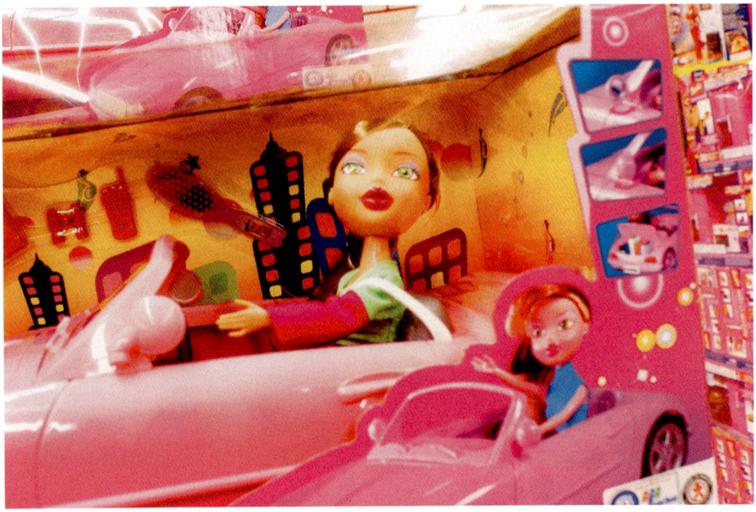

Oliviero Toscani, *Neonata,* 1992
Edward Rozzo, from *Choices*, 2003

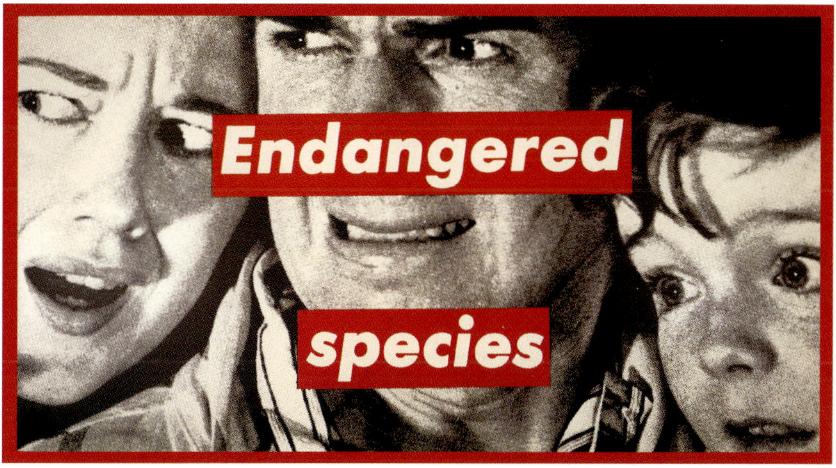

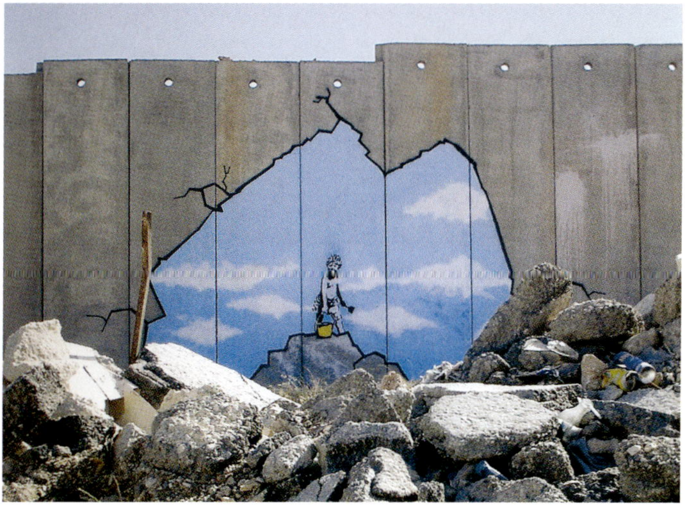

Barbara Kruger, *Untitled,* 1987
Banksy, *Ramallah Checkpoint,* 2005

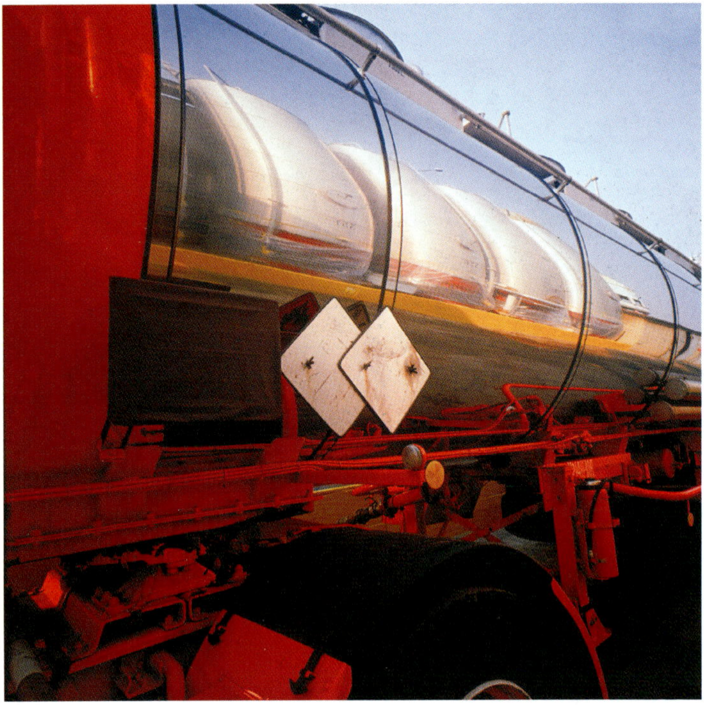

Edward Rozzo, *Chemical Tank Truck*, 1982

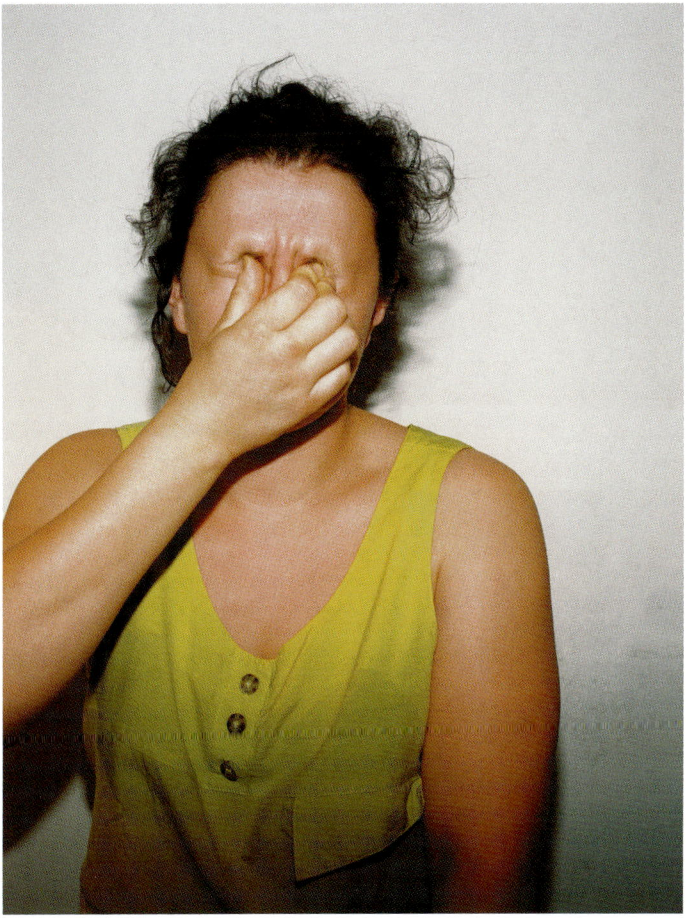

Edward Rozzo, from *What's wrong?,* 1999-2004

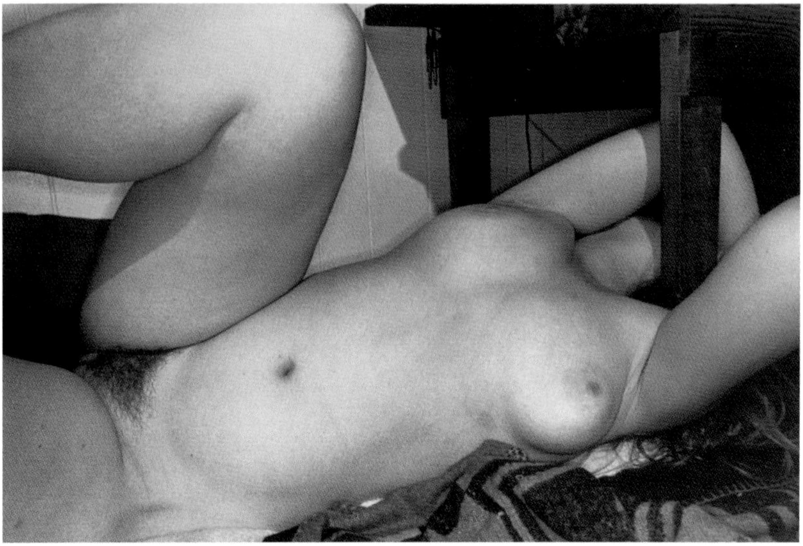

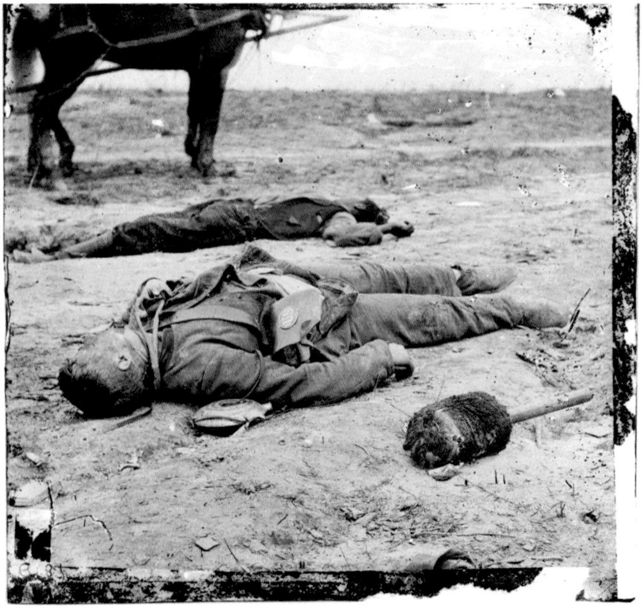

Lee Friedlander, from *Nudes*, 1976-1991
Matthew Brady, *Dead in the trenches at Fort Mahone,* c.1864

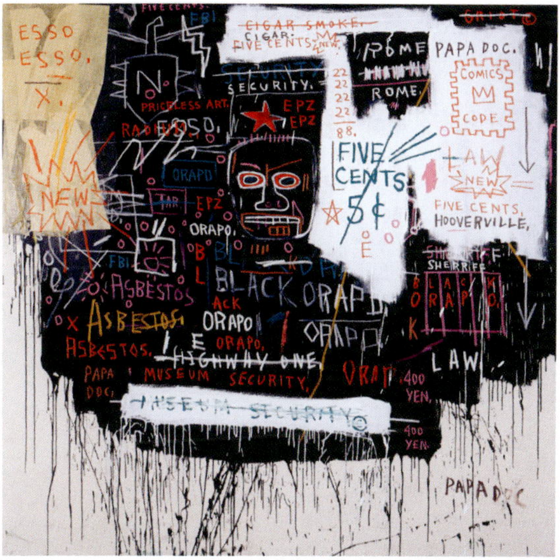

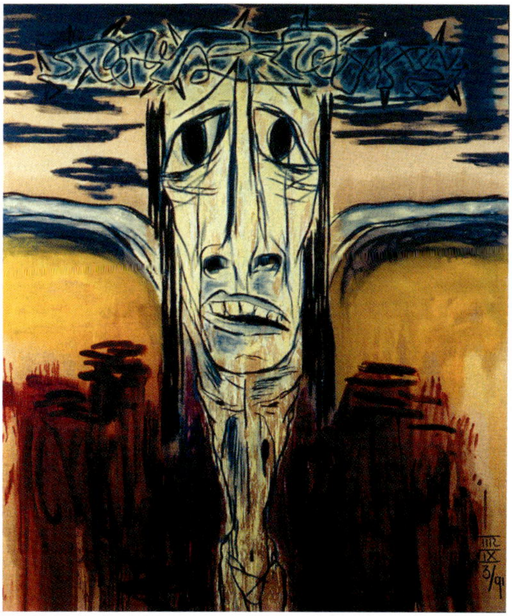

Jean-Michel Basquiat, *Museum Security*, 1983
Marcus Reichert, *Crucifixion IX*, 1991

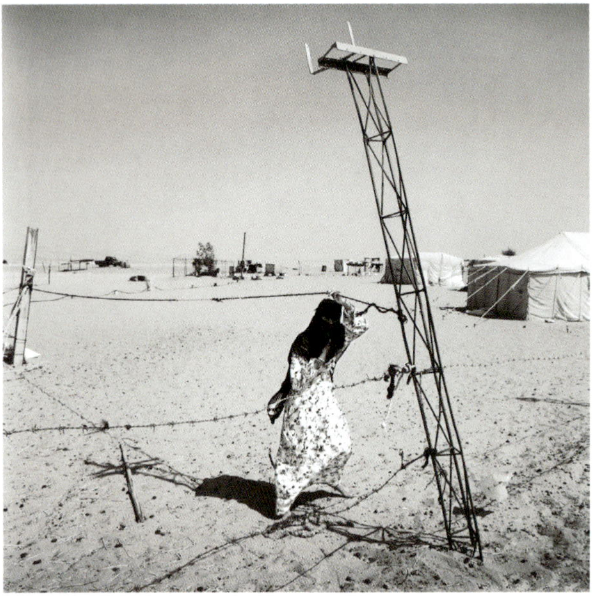

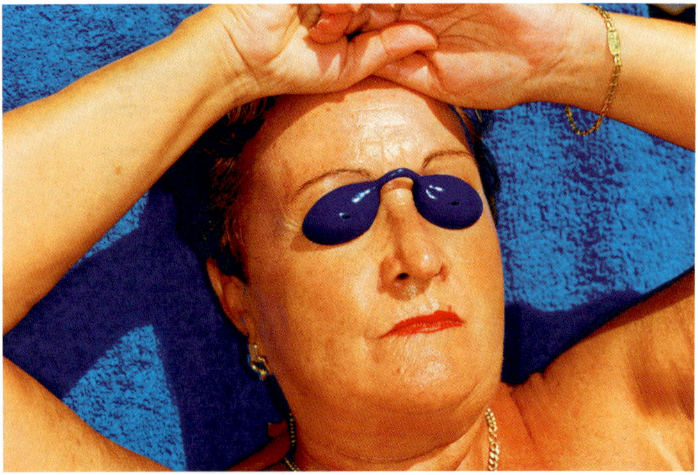

Samer Mohdad, *Saudi Arabia, The Empty Quarter*, 2005
Martin Parr, from *Common Sense,* 1995-1999

11.

MR: In an interview[21] I did with D.A. Blyler, there was the following exchange:

"Blyler: The aspect of your photographic work that I find most refreshing is its lack of any overtly moralistic, political, or sociological stance. So often in today's art we find such posturing almost obligatory. In a sense this posturing appears to be a reaction to what many people might refer to as the "egocentricity" of art, but you make no bones about the fact that the subject matter of your photographs is entirely egocentric. Do you believe artists have a moral imperative to create socially relevant work?

Reichert: Yes, perhaps we do have such an obligation, but fulfilling that obligation can take myriad unanticipated, and, occasionally, unprecedented forms. I am very uncomfortable with art that hovers anywhere near propaganda. Take Picasso's *Guernica*, this is a work profoundly sensitive to the suffering wrought by Franco and his Nazi cohorts, however there is nothing explicitly political about the painting itself. It is a work, in the suffering depicted, of great spirituality. This is its real power. Poussin's *The Rape of the Sabine Women*, Gericault's *The Raft of the Medusa*, and Matthew Brady's photographs of America's Civil War dead also come to mind. All of these works address cataclysmic human suffering with admirable formality and invention. Picasso's genius was to bring cubism into this arena of social consciousness and personal empathy. But these are pictures that deal with tragedy, they are not pictures that express a kind of social bitterness. Although I would welcome the chance to take photographs in the midst of such pathos, I have so far restricted myself to the pathos intrinsic to what I see as beauty. Taking a particular kind of photograph now means risking one's life, or worse."

---

[21] Conversation from the Margins, *Displaced Person: Poetry, Pornography & Politics*, Marcus Reichert, Ziggurat Books, London, 2006

It is apparent to me that you have given the issue of "socially relevant work" much more thought than I have. I also know that you have put your life at risk and suffered serious injury due to your unflinching commitment to doing the very best work you could in spite of the dangerous circumstances in which photographs had to be taken. This was commercial work, but commercial work involving machinery, experimental aircraft, searing heat, etc. is akin to work carried out in a war zone. Obviously, feeling some moral obligation to put one's self at risk in a politically charged situation is a very personal matter.

My problem with the idea of being *concerned* as a photographer, or even a painter, is that I don't really trust the motivating force behind it. Anger, it is agreed by many, has been the catalyst for much great writing, and here I refer to fiction and poetry as opposed to journalism. Anger, I believe, has an undeniable integrity, although as a source of inspiration it may not produce very agreeable results. When one combines the emotion of anger with that of horror, a fuller picture begins to emerge. It would be very difficult to say which photographic images of human violence and its degradation might have been inspired by anger. Often, a sense of being horrified is apparent, because it is communicated with such immediacy. Again, anger is much more difficult to read in the image.

I don't believe this is as true of painting, especially because the subject matter and how it is treated speak volumes about the painter's state of mind. Israel's indiscriminate missile attacks on the Lebanon in 2006 enraged me, as did America and Britain's unwillingness to intercede. We were bombarded on television (in Europe) with images of the slaughter and mutilation of hundreds of innocent people, people who were trapped in their neighbourhoods, forbidden by Israeli force to leave the killing-zone. Beirut, which had taken years to restore after the last war, was hit again and again for no good reason. I found myself in my studio one afternoon painting a Lebanese woman in a smart dress, the kind of woman who might work in an office in Beirut, with blood pouring from her eyes. Certainly there were still photographers and television crews that were possessed of the same outrage. A few of the reporters who were obliged to address the camera each day clearly evidenced their loathing for the wanton destruction they were obliged to witness. So, being 'concerned' might not be nearly as helpful when recording man's inhumanity to man as being angry.

ER: For me, being *concerned* doesn't necessarily mean taking images that are atrocious in a war zone. Also your comments about one's anger with respect to atrocities brings to mind a very amusing series that the famous British graffiti artist Banksy did in Palestine. He painted beautiful vacation landscapes on the wall separating Israel from the Palestinian territories: as if by poking a hole in the wall, you could reach some kind of Paradise. Given the situation in that and other Middle Eastern countries, he really put his finger into the sore which touches both sides in a tragic way. But his actual work was a joke. Was this joke less concerned than desperate images of war victims? I don't think so.

Of course, giving vent to your anger doesn't necessarily provoke an intelligent reaction. For that reason, I appreciate the work of Banksy, and Martin Parr. They're showing us faults and errors in our society without necessarily pointing the finger at one side or the other. Everyone involved *thinks* he's on the right side, that's what makes these conflicts so devastating. Then there's the question of the role violence occupies in society. I think there's an important relation between how near one is to real violence (slaughtering of animals, natural disasters, etc.) and the abstraction of violence that we have on television and in movies. The line between real and perceived violence is a very dangerous one.

MR: This brings us to an earlier discussion we had in which I said that I am now convinced that the pleasure people take in the anticipation of violence will continue to infect the future. It would seem that the "surge of anxiety which fills the present" is unavoidable, felt publicly and privately, and a direct result of the inevitability of, firstly, death and, secondly, the haphazard destruction meted out by humanity. Although visual expressions of this void would also seem inevitable, your research and exposition of this state strikes me as uncanny, especially when so many artists are striving so mightily to find some palatable universal expression of their existence. But of course thousands of "artists" are also employed in the creation of special EFX for feature films that feed this appetite for violence, and it now seems to be verging on gluttony. I don't consider myself squeamish, although I do have a difficult time watching surgery on TV, but frankly I am often unnerved by the weird thrill I experience when watching cataclysmic destruction in dramatic films. This is not a morbid fascination, as I imagine pornography is for some people, but it *is* some sort of primordial reaction that perhaps has to do with humanity's death wish.

ER: I think pornography, including war imagery, is a cheap thrill that distorts one's relationship with the world. It's a negative experience doled out as a hot trick. Kill 'em, fuck 'em, eat 'em. It's simply barbarity. Why not put war atrocity photographs on the Coca Cola cups at McDonald's? Or pictures of women with their legs spread on pizza boxes?

MR: What if you were asked to take pictures in a war zone, would you consider doing this at all? And, if you were, on what terms and conditions?

ER: If I were asked to take pictures in a war zone, I'd be pretty careful where and on whose side. I don't get thrills putting my life at risk—I have two kids, a wife, a lot of responsibility. If I could magically be in a war zone with low risk, I'd try and show the daily normalness of the people involved. I'd try to show that both sides have the same people on them, but they don't realise it. But that's a philosophical answer to your question and not a real one. I wouldn't go to a war zone, I don't think it's worth the risk.

MR: I'd have to say that I feel about the same, both in terms of creative motivation and my instinct for self-preservation. I can however appreciate that if ordinary life was for some reason impossible to bear and the possibility of suicide had become a dominant presence in one's thoughts, putting one's life at risk to reveal the suffering that war brings could be a transforming experience, in one of two ways. The trick would be not to wind up disabled or horribly disfigured, like so many casualties of war. But I do absolutely see the moral value in showing what goes on with one's photographs. By the way, I don't see anything the matter with getting paid well for this kind of work, not when billions and billions are spent wrecking the world and people's lives for one insane reason or another.

I'm curious to know why you find photographs of people destroyed by warfare unworthy of consideration, but you did find Maurizio Catalan's instillation of the lynching of children in the plaza in Milano worthy of your artistic appreciation? Why, as you said before, is it OK for an artist to show the atrocities of war and not the media?

ER: One has got to distinguish between playing on people's emotion and playing on their intellect. Catalan makes you think and reflect by shocking you visually and conceptually. Images of the atrocities of war appeal to the basic instinct of animal aggressiveness. It's great to be on the winning side and see what damage happens to the other side—the wrong side. But I think that's bullshit. Everyone is usually on the wrong side and the right side at the same time. That's why wars are so horrendous, they confuse identities in order to control people, nations, states. Any normal person wants to live in peace and not be bullied around. That's—in a very comic strip sort of way—the basis for America as a nation. That's the basis for modern democracies. But real life is more complex than that, so there are conflicts. Conflicts happen all the time, even between any two people. On that scale, you can already see the alternatives: give and take until you understand and accept each other's differences, or one of you beats the shit out of the other, because one of you is stronger. Unfortunately, some politicians aren't up to the give and take relationship.

MR: Before we move on to the subject of pornography per se, I'm curious to know if you think there might be some correlation between the anger I often feel when viewing images of warfare, and especially the so-called collateral damage inflicted on innocent people, and the anger that might very well be at the root of violent aggression on the societal or national level. My response to my own anger can be to make an extremely violent painting or take an almost grotesquely bleak photograph. Do you have any thoughts on this?

ER: Anger and/or indignation certainly are a motivating force. They bring one's instinct for rebellion to some constituted order. But the results are also fairly uncontrollable. It's part of today's egocentric identity: if I feel it must be right, then it must be healthy for me to act on it. That, in my opinion, is bullshit. Controlling one's emotions has a lot to do with maturity, but we seem to have lost that part of the equation. We're stuck only with: don't show your weak side, don't show your pain. As to anger being the reason to destroy and conquer—bullshit.

MR: Yes, but it's pain that triggers my anger, and it's this pain that is evident in the painting that is the result of this violent reaction. Perhaps that is the value in such a work of art—the pain that hopefully the artist shares with the viewer. OK, so what if you were asked to take pictures of two people involved sexually?

ER: It's not the kind of subject matter that interests me as an observer. Let's just say, I'd rather be in the picture than taking it. I'm not saying that certain images aren't beautiful or significant. I can think of one of Nan Goldin's images of a couple making love that is quite strong. But you see, sex as depicted in that image, I feel, is an interesting subject because it's rooted in deeper issues than sexual excitement. Sex is the motor for a lot of profound communication. Making erotic pictures, though, is not really my line of business. I like a hands-on reality and not a conceptual one. I think fashion photography is far more interesting. It's a mixture of commercial tease and social comment combined in an almost perverse way. It reveals problems of identity and roots. It reflects the individual's desire to emerge and declare a sexual identity, whatever that may be, and it's almost unconsciously about politics. Fashion photography calls out with provocation and allure. It's like the sirens of Greek mythology. Fashion is somehow always calling you into her spell with either imagined perfection or provocative arrogance, somehow always trying to catch a piece of your imaginary identity and give it a boost. It's a fascinating exchange which interests me immensely. For me, fashion is the concrete visualisation of the most subtle inner feelings about one's self. It's like visual psychoanalysis.

MR: It's curious that you, whose photographs are so very different to mine, should have a similar fascination with fashion as a subject. My father went from being a portrait painter into advertising when he found it impossible to provide for a wife and three children on two or three commissions a year. He had been the art director for the US Navy's enlistment program during WWII and had an uncanny knack for coming up with good campaigns, so creating his own advertising studio was rather a nostalgic adventure. At any event, he began bringing home copies of Vogue Magazine and Harper's Bazaar and I found them very intriguing and very sexy. Later, when he got the Christian Dior hosiery account for the US, the selection of the models his studio would work with became my secret obsession.

My affection was always for the least orthodox face and figure, which is of course the direction discovering models has gone in over the years. When, at the age of 21, I married Sally MacLeod, she wasn't a model but very easily could have been, and later was. Wilhelmina and then Askew's sent her all over the world, and I would occasionally chase after her. We had an especially divine rendezvous in your city of Milano, and it was there, after a modelling shoot with Sally still in her make-up, that I took some of my most memorable pictures of her. That's the essential background to what follows.

When, in fashion photography or fine art photography, you have a subject with whom you are enamoured, exceptional things can happen—one example being Jean Shrimpton and David Bailey, another being Georgia O'Keefe and Alfred Steiglitz. It's the intimacy that brings the beauty of the moment and the psychology of that relationship into focus. I may be stating the obvious but this sort of collaboration doesn't come around every day. I know you can appreciate this because your pictures of Kristin Helberg, your then wife, are intimate but also uncannily formal in a lyrical, dare I say, existentialist sort of way. My photographs of Sally were never meant to be published or exhibited—because I wasn't a proper photographer, let alone a proper fashion photographer—but the clandestine aspect of photographing her nearly naked in public places like Holland Park in London is now acknowledged to have been prescient. These photographs are fragile things for me because our private exploitation of each other is apparent.

ER: I really don't know what to say about this aspect of my photography. It's true, I did take many photographs of Kristin. I was influenced, of course, by Harry Callahan who was my teacher. But I never convinced myself that these images were more than wonderful pictures of my wife. So, you might say, it was due to my immaturity that I didn't continue with this kind of work. With later girlfriends, wives, and lovers, I never got into photographing any of them in a very special way. Marianne, my present wife, has often been the object of my photographic interests. But since I'm less interested in showing the erotically perfect side of life than in showing the distressingly realistic side, my subject, whoever she is, eventually refuses to be photographed, or refuses to allow the work I've done to be shown.

MR: You mentioned Nan Goldin as someone who takes very strong pictures of people making love. Beyond what I consider the compelling beauty of many of her images, she has the uncanny ability to bring a weird haphazardness into play which gives a quiet, disarming depth to the subject. Somehow, she manages to capture people and places together in a kind of collusion which I identify with enormously. Nan Goldin and I had a friend in common, Cookie Mueller, with whom I spent many an endearingly desolate night in New York. I first saw Cookie acting in a film by Amos Poe and found her very sexy. Amos and I were both struggling to make films and so we appreciated each other's particular dilemmas. At any event, Cookie and I eventually met and we spent quite a lot of time alone together, and occasionally in the company of her young son Max. Cookie used to leave New York for days at a time. She used to go to northern Africa with a few of her chums and shoot heroin. She had Berber tattoos on her fingers and shared a needle.

In 1989, Cookie died of AIDS at the age of 40. Her husband Vittorio also died of AIDS due to his own addiction to heroin. Nan Goldin's *Ten Years After* is a kind of gentle exposé of the life Cookie and Vittorio shared. These are supremely melancholy images that have an almost otherworldly fatality about them. But Goldin's work with Cookie carried on until Cookie was dead. These images of Cookie's transformation from vibrant woman to waxen object of fascination were shown at the Whitney Museum and, by all accounts, were harrowing. Cookie may have been reckless but she also had courage. She and Nan Goldin made a statement. I've never been able to look at these photographs. If I were outraged by Nan Goldin's willingness to photograph Cookie dying it would be one thing, but I'm not. I'm just too much of a coward to see Cookie's suffering frozen before me. Somehow I think it would have been easier to be there.

12.

ER: Are we all artists? In our globalised world of shifting social and cultural values, the emphasis is decidedly on the freedom we have as individuals to express ourselves as we please, when we please, in any way that doesn't conflict with someone else's interests. You might say we're approaching cultural anarchy—anything goes and my taste has the same value as yours. After all, we're all consumers. Or should I say, we're all artistic consumers of our own identity. It's a frightful thought.

MR: Yes, this casts doubt on the proposition of being an artist. And it makes the task of expressing what poetry there is in the world and in our lives even more difficult. It has always been essential in some small way that a poet strike a pose, that he assume the character of his work. He was often an object of derision. Most people believed that being a poet was not a proper job for anybody, however these same people took joy in the spiritual gratification provided by the poet's labours. The proposition of being a poet has been romanticised and, much worse, democratised, so that, as you say, now anyone can play at being an artist.

ER: It's like our egos are exploding in space and will continue to explode in space until someone comes along and, against our will, constructs a wall to contain us. Then we're really fucked. But is everyone *really* an artist? Or has everyone simply claimed the right to express themselves? Are we now like a bunch of kids taking a bath together?

MR: It would appear that this is very much the case. As I said before, the artist produces the ingredients that are now manipulated by the operatives of a vast bureaucratic scheme. I'm not paranoid. Anyone with any cultural wherewithal whatsoever knows that art has become a viable form of mass entertainment, and Tate Modern is the Disneyland of so-called fine art. It's very big business. There's nothing sinister in this, unless of course one regards the dilution of poetry and thought to make it more appealing to the public a form of degeneration. It strikes me as hideously ironic that the Nazis did their best to destroy German art of the modernist and expressionist movements when today virtually anything that is promoted effectively passes for modern art, but more exactly art that expresses the artist's relevance within the bureaucratic scheme of things.

ER: Yes, when moral and ethical guidelines are forged through cultural masturbation—everyone just loves the latest album, theatrical piece, film, new emerging artist—until we all feel a healthy orgasm of self-justification. Are we now a political entity of "ethical" intellectuals trying to navigate the limits of narcissistic anarchy? Has visual expression replaced religion? Has art become a way of sharing the guilt, anxiety, and pain of living? Is it like group therapy? Is it something to decorate our walls with while our walls become moving images of virtual emotions?

MR: It seems to me that we are consumed by our own exquisite personalities as manifest in our art. Everything around us must be a manifestation of our sensibility, and that manifestation had better have impact. Our identity has become our *ultimate* work of art, but only if we can get it across convincingly and—here's the best part—with technological proficiency. And we aren't talking about anything as mundane as achievement or as inept as personal style, we're talking about the technology of the new aesthetics. We're talking about the infallible incandescence of celebrity. Yes, moving images of virtual emotions shall triumph. That is, until virtual emotions become passé and everyone learns how to cry on cue, which is coming.

ER: I believe in late modernity more than post modernity. That means I believe that things can become better. The ignorant youth isn't *simply* ignorant. The consumerist wasteland of western society isn't *simply* a wasteland. I have faith. The faith of Thomas Aquinas, the faith of Plutarch. Our secular society is not without a spiritual basis, it's just difficult to find it, especially amongst the commercial vultures who govern most of our daily consumption. We've still got a long way to go, but I think visual expression, understanding ideas through colours, forms, etc. is a kind of psychotherapy—a *visual* psychotherapy. It is a form of confession, a very private confession between ourselves and a communal sense of self.

MR: I don't share your faith, because I see mankind committing the same acts of cruelty again and again. What you say about visual psychotherapy however does make perfect sense to me. It really is at the subliminal core of my painting. I can't say the same is true of my photographs, because the photographs are only obliquely about exposing my psyche to myself. I look at the photographs and I am nearly convinced that what I see before me is what I know, or what I knew when I took the photograph. As objects, photographs are mysterious and elusive things in themselves. My paintings are about something else altogether. They very often are painted in a kind of trance. What occurs on the canvas is coming from a place I can't reach in any other way. In fact, there is no known logic to this sequence of events. Yes, it is a form of confession but that confession is written in a language that is not immediately decipherable. It takes me a while to understand what I've put on the canvas and then, either I eventually move on to a second state, or the painting is complete.

ER: But that, I think, is the beauty of this new kind of confession. It's *not* evident, it doesn't lose its meaning after the next yawn or commercial. It *does* take time to understand, but that's its beauty. It's a new way to get in touch with, as you say, a place one can't reach in any other way. That's what spirituality has always been about. That's why I believe in this *second coming* in the form of art, design, and culture. It's already here, but we're not aware of it yet. Most people haven't been pulled into the revelation. Getting back to your painting, I think understanding your work is about understanding some very subtle and sometimes disturbing things. It's about contemplation. I wish people looked at photographs in the same way, but they don't. They simply flip through the pages and say something like, "Oh look, what a boring street corner." At least people look at a painting *knowing* that it's not easy to see.

MR: But it's not a new way, it's a very old way. Good painting has always been about this. Painters as diverse as Henri Matisse and Jackson Pollock are about this. Sentimental painting, the kind of paintings people make in prison or of their girlfriends and boyfriends, is very much about this. There are confessional works of art and there are *disarmingly confessional* works of art. The portraits that Antonin Artaud drew near the end of his life at La Maison de Santé d'Ivry were about shared confession. His subjects allowed him to probe their faces and their psyches in a way that is almost painfully intimate. Artaud's drawings of his friends are frightening in that they are so bleak and yet so opulent in their detail. His eyes rove over the pores of his subject's flesh as his mind roves over the landscape of his subject's soul. I can't think of any other way to put it. Artaud opens up the person before us and enables us to see what he sees. His subjects had courage.

ER: You mentioned the technology of the new aesthetics, which is very much about personal expression and visibility. By now, we can see what's coming: images everywhere, all the time, fluidly on our person, on walls, in empty space. We'll be connected to the internet and similar real-time globalised webs 24 hours a day. We already live outside the space-time continuum of our fathers. We're getting ready for the ubiquitous self. The problem is that most people are victims of *image culture*. I think the real problem in the future globalised world will be visual illiteracy. Visual art is *pure* communication, like music. It allows people to get in touch with themselves, with problems bigger than themselves. That's all good. Unfortunately, the vast majority of viewers are totally visually illiterate. Some think they understand because they can *recognise* subject matter, others because they can identify some classical school of thought. Beyond that, they see nothing.

MR: I watch people in my studio, I see how they react to something alien to their everyday lives. I wait for the atmosphere to envelope them, I wait for the viewer to be possessed by some strange sensation. When I walk into another artist's studio, I experience the same thing. The same transforming sensation. Occasionally, nothing happens, but usually there is something about the thought circulating in that place that either penetrates my own thinking or that I reject. It's about being pervaded, perhaps even consumed by another sensibility. It's a marvellous thing to experience, especially when it's your own work that is generating this sequence of revelations. I think people who are serious about experiencing visual art are willing to momentarily leave themselves behind. For me, there is too much art that flatters the viewer with his presence on the earth, with his importance as judge and jury in the *artworld* melodrama. I like to think that my pictures require a kind of selflessness to be appreciated.

ER: That's why I teach. It's like being a prophet in the desert: no one is looking for you, no one thinks you've got anything interesting to say. We've all got something interesting to say, but we've got to say it to each other. That's why the role of art is changing. Rightly so. We all should have the possibility to express ourselves in various forms, but whoever chooses to dedicate his life to making images should be regarded as someone who is meditating on the meaning of life.

MR: That, I think, is the sense of responsibility that we acknowledge to ourselves when we are looking at something that we find worthwhile. But I'm not at all certain we all have something interesting to say, at least not visually. There is the joy of expressing one's self visually, and we see this joy especially in children's drawings and paintings. But we also see it in almost anything created visually by someone who is excited by the experience. I've worked as a visiting studio critic in painting and the difference in people's attitudes to their work can be shocking. The difference of course lies in who regards the effort of making a picture as a privilege and who regards it as a job. I often wonder why someone wants to make a career of painting when that career is tantamount to employment by an unacknowledged corporation, the corporation of successful art. It's the idea of being a successful artist and therefore a celebrity that runs contrary to what making images is meant to be about. Whosoever meditates on the meaning of life through his images is blessed.

ER: And like any mystical experience, some people get it, some don't, and some fantasise about it via projections of themselves in an auto-referential way. I don't know what the role of art is in society because art is no longer an established group of things that people do. Some still think art is exclusively painting and sculpture, others think it's photography and video too. My roots lie in what I consider to be the evident meaning of a series of writings by Anada Coomaraswamy[22] in the 1930's and 40's while he was the Curator of Indian Art at the Boston Museum of Fine Arts. He said: Art is not the object, it's the process. Once you've grasped that, the world opens up and you no longer categorise what art is and what art isn't. It's the process, it's the way you do things. Whether you're painting a painting or building a table, what enriches the object is the artistry you used in making it.

MR: I think a lot of what we've been talking about throughout these discussions has to do with just this. Simon Lane[23] made an astute observation about our current predicament, he said:

"In the same way in which visiting card printers suggest limits to their clients' profession(s) for reasons of space or indolence—"Phrenologist, Philanthropist, Phantasist"—society

---

[22] Published by South Asia Books as *Christian and Oriental Philosophy of Art* by Anada Coomaraswamy

[23] The Light of Thought (Introduction), *Displaced Person: Poetry, Pornography & Politics*, Marcus Reichert, Ziggurat Books, London, 2006

tends to look askance at those who confess to a multiplicity of talent. In earlier times, the polymath was two to a penny: a doctor was a botanist, a parson a poet, a poet a soldier. These days, not so, for we have evolved, or devolved, into the specialist. If it was tolerable for James Joyce to strum his banjo (in private) then it was always considered slightly pretentious of Paul Bowles or Anthony Burgess to compose music as well as fiction. More's the pity."

This harkens back to my belief that all of it is about finding poetry in the world. Depending upon the visceral extremity of the subject, that poetry may be horrific and excruciating to experience but it is nevertheless the manifestation of a sensibility—the artist's sensibility—in pursuit of meaning, no matter how abstract or elusive that meaning might be. We've certainly agreed that the meaning is often in the experience of the thing. When Simon mentions Joyce strumming his banjo, it's fascinating to imagine the same mind finding an harmonious (or discordant) order in the rhythms of his words on the page. There is a discipline to this process in any medium which is very difficult to grasp. Although it certainly hinges on the ego for much of its impetus, the compulsion to find or distil an imagery that in any way communicates what we want to communicate is necessarily a process of refinement, at least in the way our minds struggle towards an imagery that possesses an undeniable resonance. This may sound terribly complex, but it's actually quite simple: it's about finding the inexplicable meaning in what we see.

ER: You might call it finding poetry, I'd rather call it finding oneself through what one does. It might be visual art or it might be a craft. If you do it with your mind *and* your emotions, you produce objects that reflect not only yourself but some part of everyone else. It's about finding meaning, like you said. I totally agree.

MR: Something has been pestering me which we might discuss: extreme identification with one's self and what this has to do with making images. I often worry that any image I make is totally irrelevant because I made it. At the same time, I argue with myself that whatever image I make, if made with integrity, might at least be of some subliminal consequence for the viewer. I openly admit that the reason I paint is to demonstrate to myself that I am actually alive, but that may be an attendant aspect of my particular psychosis. I sometimes wonder if when a person commits an unbelievably violent crime if that person is not at the time finding the only way he knows to project himself into some sort of reality. I wonder if when we make an image, by taking a photograph or making a painting, we aren't similarly projecting ourselves into what subconsciously we consider a forbidden reality.

ER: Often we are driven by influences we can't control, like our parents' attitudes and habits, like childhood traumas. These are *ready-made* compulsions. We're constructing our sense of *self*. This is what we're doing when we desire and buy something we feel is essential to our own way of living. How much is projection, how much is conscientious projection, how much is pathological projection? This is a rather delicate question.

MR: Albert Camus' character Meursault kills a man on the beach apparently without motive. His mother had died the day before, or some other day. Meursault doesn't keep track of time very well. *The Outsider* begins as a kind of hallucination. For me, I was convinced by the book, and my own experience, that life is an hallucination. We're never really certain why Meursault kills the stranger, except that the man was going to die anyway. We can kill any living thing at any irrelevant moment in our lives. But what does this mean? Even in its unbearable slowness, life is violent. Sometimes when we make a work of art, I believe, we are objectifying our violence, our anger. Life can be a horribly frustrating proposition. Perhaps sometimes it's this violence one needs to experience to bring one's tenderness, one's pathos into focus.

ER: But not everyone has the same frustrations to vent. In part we express ourselves to communicate, in part we express ourselves to alleviate some deep feelings, in part we express ourselves to show ourselves that we've done something worth looking at. It's like attributing meaning to things. In any society you can only attribute meaning to things which everyone agrees upon, otherwise they're just random meanings which negate the hermeneutic process of attributing meanings.

MR: We have to project new meanings which initially appear to be nonsensical. It's how intellectually we evolve.

ER: They don't mean anything to anyone else but you.

MR: Frankly, I don't care if anyone understands what I'm saying when I say it. They can and will understand later, or perhaps not. We are programmed to live and express ourselves selfishly. It's only when we bring the mirror up close that nearly everyone sees the same thing.

8th May to 10th August 2007
Milano / St. Hippolyte du Fort

REPRODUCTION CREDITS
Drawings, Paintings, and Photographs

Marcus Reichert, *Sally MacLeod, London*, 1979
© Marcus Reichert, courtesy of the artist

David Douglas Duncan, *Picasso, Mougins*, 1962
© David Douglas Duncan, courtesy of the artist and the Harry Ransom Humanities Research Center, University of Texas at Austin

Nan Goldin, *Skinhead having sex, London*, 1978
© Nan Goldin, courtesy of the artist

William Eggleston, *Untitled (Memphis, Tennessee)*, 2000
© Copyright 2007 Eggleston Artistic Trust, courtesy of Cheim & Read, New York. Used with permission. All rights reserved.

Marcus Reichert, *Drawing-room, Ramsgate*, 2002
© Marcus Reichert, courtesy of the artist

Amos Chan, *Union City* (production still), 1979
© Marcus Reichert, courtesy of Marcus Reichert & Co. and the Museum of Modern Art, New York

Marcus Reichert, *Lampman*, 2007
© Marcus Reichert, courtesy of the artist

Richard Avedon, *Dick Hickock, murderer, Garden City, Kansas, April 15, 1960*
© 2008 The Richard Avedon Foundation

Antonin Artaud, *Portrait of Mania Oïfer*, 1947
© Estate of Antonin Artaud, courtesy of Paule Thévenin

Piers Faccini, *Head of Antonin Artaud*, 1990
© Piers Faccini, courtesy of the artist

Marcus Reichert, *Woman's Head in Green*, 2002–2004
© Marcus Reichert, courtesy of the artist

Edward Rozzo, from *Urgent Stories*, 1990–2000
© Edward Rozzo, courtesy of the artist

Photographer unknown, *Peter Beard and Isak Dinesen, Denmark*, 1961 – courtesy of Peter Beard

Francis Bacon, *Dog*, 1952
© Estate of Francis Bacon, courtesy of Faggionato Fine Art, London

Philip-Lorca diCorcia, *New York*, 1997
© Philip-Lorca diCorcia, courtesy of the artist and Pace/MacGill Gallery, New York

Brassaï, *Washing up in a brothel, Rue Quincampoix*, c.1932
© Estate of Brassaï, courtesy of Gilberte Brassaï

Oliviero Toscani, *Neonata*, 1992
© Copyright 1991 Benetton Group S.p.A., courtesy of Benetton Group S.p.A.

Edward Rozzo, from *Choices*, 2003
© Edward Rozzo, courtesy of the artist

Barbara Kruger, *Untitled*, 1987
© Barbara Kruger, courtesy of Mary Boone Gallery, New York

Bansky, *Ramallah Checkpoint*, 2005
© Bansky, photographer unknown

Edward Rozzo, *Chemical Tank Truck*, 1982
© Edward Rozzo, courtesy of the artist

Edward Rozzo, from *What's wrong?*, 1999–2004
© Edward Rozzo, courtesy of the artist

Lee Freidlander, *Nude*, 1975
© Lee Freidlander, courtesy of Janet Borden Inc., New York

Matthew Brady, *Dead in the trenches at Fort Mahone*, c.1864
© Library of Congress, Prints & Photographs Division, 1977.
No. 0425 [Matthew Brady-LC-DIG-cwpb-02550 DLC]

Jean-Michel Basquiat, *Museum Security*, 1983
© Estate of Jean-Michel Basquiat, courtesy of Faggionato Fine Art, London

Marcus Reichert, *Crucifixion IX*, 1991
© Marcus Reichert, courtesy of the artist

Samer Mohdad, *Saudi Arabia, The Empty Quarter*, 2005
© Samer Mohdad, courtesy of the artist

Martin Parr, from *Common Sense*, 1995–1999
© Martin Parr, courtesy of the artist and Magnum, London